Dying
to
Survive

the Ed Buck story

Ed and Micki Buck
with memories by
Clara Hammie, RN

Published by

Jawbone Publishing corporation
1540 W. Happy Valley Circle
Newnan, GA 30263-4065
www.JawbonePublishing.com
678-854-8620

Printed in the United States of America

ISBN 1-59094-153-5

Dedication

We would like to dedicate this book to all the people who made it possible for us to survive this tragic accident. From all the personnel in the different hospitals to Delmarva Power and its employees to our town and neighbors who made us keep trying. We would also like to dedicate this book to Swanee Ballman who is not only our publisher but a dear friend who has shown us so much care, encouragement and love. She is one is a million! And last but not least, we would like to thank Ester Ball for proofreading this book. you are fantastic! Thank you all.

Foreword

As I Remember

Within the pages of this book, I will attempt to paint pictures with words. These words are my honest effort to describe events of the past 40 years, starting with July 27, 1967, the day before I experienced the most radical change of my life.

July 27 sets the groundwork for what is to follow—so many small and unnoticeable events... routine happenings that create the potential for disaster.

July 28, 1967 was the day my family's world changed forever from a peaceful, loving, hard working-class environment to pain, suffering and tears. Decisions had to be made without any knowledge of what the future would bring. An entire neighborhood would rally to help one young family understand the meaning of friendship and love for one another. The outstandingly loyal company with whom I had the privilege of working, along with the employees—many of whom I had not met—made such a difference in my life and the lives of my family, I will never be able to thank them enough.

This book includes the different stages of recovery from hell (yes, the events I will describe can honestly be considered hell). I apologize in advance for some of the gory things I will relate to you; but in order for you to understand the whole story and my survival, it is necessary.

The long and painful recovery process—coupled with the many prayers, contributions both monetary and physical—made it impossible to stop trying to live. The great amount of love, assistance and opportunity that I have received over the past 40 years will reveal how I/we have adapted to complex adverse conditions. This in its entirety is why I was......

Dying to Survive

The Day Before

Thursday, July 27, 1967 was a normal day in the small town of Fruitland, Maryland. Hazy, hot and humid was the forecast. The central portion of the Delmarva Peninsula—consisting of Delaware, Maryland, and Virginia's Eastern shore—were subject to these conditions due to its location between the Atlantic Ocean to the East and the Chesapeake Bay to the West.

The alarm sounded at the normal time for me, 6:30 AM. And while my wife, Micki, fixed breakfast, I got dressed. Then I woke our two little boys, Danny, five, and Robbie, two, and got them dressed after a small pillow fight. (Mommy yelled in the background,) "If you burst those pillows, you will have a mess to clean up!" as she laughed.

Those memories are here to stay.

After our breakfast and the usual goodbye kisses and hugs, I left for work. On the way I listened again to the forecast on our car radio: 80% chance of late afternoon thunderstorms, again not an unusual forecast for that time of year.

I arrived at my place of employment, where I had been an apprentice lineman for almost 3 years. Delmarva Power and Light is the largest electric company on the whole Peninsula. At that time I was 25 years old, almost 6 feet two inches tall and weighed 227 pounds.

I was in the best physical condition I had ever been. This played a big part in the events.

I worked in one of the two crews based in the southern division general office building, located in Salisbury, Maryland. Our start time was 8 a.m. and most of the crew arrived between 7:30 and 7:45 AM.

We assembled on what was known as the loading dock. This was where all line trucks, both distribution and station crews parked their vehicles for the night...to keep them out of the weather. Inclement conditions are hazardous to working on energized electrical equipment.

Shortly before 8:00 our foreman, Oscar Martin, came on the loading dock with the work location and orders for that day. We were going to a Berlin, Maryland substation, where we would unload breakers (which are used in the substation for switching) and would be stored until they were needed. This was going to be a two-day job.

On this day three vehicles went. One was an auto car, a 1940s vintage line truck so beat up and dented that the canopy which covered the compartment that held our ropes and hand-held equipment would not shut. Next was a "White" (manufacturer's name for a 1950's vintage line truck) that had just been refurbished at the White factory, with a new hydraulic boom to replace an old and outdated telescopic boom. (This new boom made the compartment where the ropes and handheld equipment were stored also inoperable, preventing the canopy from closing.) And third was the carryall, which was a van type vehicle which carried the rest of the crew.)

We had two trucks with canopy covers that would not close. It was a hot, humid and hazy day with 80% chance of rain in the afternoon. All these factors pointed to the potential for disaster, which neither I nor anyone else knew at that time. (Also keep in mind the ropes used for the job had been used for several months, so were old and dirty. The part about being dirty is another link in the chain of events.

The crew consisting of Oscar Martin, foreman, Landis Donaway, winch truck operator, Ben Richardson, journeyman lineman, Gene Shirk, apprentice lineman (B), Lester Lynch, ground man, and me,

Ed Buck, apprentice lineman (C) now head for Berlin to start the day's work.

I was in my third year of a four-year apprenticeship to become a journeyman lineman.

* * *

All went well with transferring the breakers. Since we knew the project couldn't be completed in one day, we cleaned up the work site. Ropes and tools were loaded back on the trucks in their proper places. (Everything on the line trucks had its own spot and was to be kept that way.)

The two hook ladders—one a 20 foot and the other a 10 foot-(just what you think…ladders with two pieces of flat steel shaped like a hook on either side) were left behind; they would not be needed in the next few days.

I was driving the auto car. Lester Lynch rode with me. Landis Donaway and Oscar Martin drove the white line truck, while Ben Richardson and Gene Shirk drove the carry-all (which, by the way, did not have a two-way radio).

As we headed toward Salisbury, the sky was turning very black, ushering in that 80% chance of rain. Lightning flashed every few seconds and the rain came down so hard visibility was almost nonexistent.

The old auto car started to misfire, although I was trying desperately to keep it running. I pulled over to the side of the road to try to keep it from choking out. I called Oscar on the radio for assistance, but however, there was no response.

After repeatedly calling the system operator, Jimmy Maurrel, in Salisbury responded. I told him my location and the conditions, but he told me he didn't know when he could get me any help.

After sitting there for quite a while, we decided to try to limp home. We pulled out on the highway and head toward Salisbury with the engine still missing. But at least we were moving, though the best we could go was about 25 or 30 miles an hour.

The trip took an hour and a half, when usually it took about 30 minutes.

* * *

We normally parked the trucks near the gas pump, so the evening shift in the transportation shop could refuel and make any repairs for the next day's work. We parked the auto car in line next to the fuel pump and stepped out into water... just below our knees. We had to wade through this water back to the loading dock so we could clock out and headed for our cars.

You can just imagine my mood as I drove home with wet feet, socks, leather boots, and jeans. I was not a happy camper. However, when I arrived at the house terribly frustrated with the end of the day, the greatest gal on this planet made it all worthwhile. She had our two little boys all cleaned up and ready to jump into daddy arms, fighting over who got picked up first.

Next I received a warm kiss from my girl, who had a delicious dinner on the table. I hate to brag, but this is what I got to come home to every night. She made sure coming home was a pleasure, something to look forward to. We seldom ate out, because our paycheck, at that time, didn't afford that luxury. (Eating out consisted of a hamburger at a fast food restaurant.)

After dinner, as Micki cleared the table, I took our two guys outside for our evening ritual of romping on the ground or playing ball, if the weather permitted. We had a great time, either way. If our post-dinner play was in the living room, we would have wrestling matches on the carpet.

That night we decided to play ball, but the puddles the rain had left in the driveway were just too inviting. After all, it was July and we didn't have a swimming pool, so running through and jumping in puddles was so much fun.

Nightfall came all too soon. Both boys were quite muddy, and baths were in order. Micki threatened us not to get her clean floors all wet in the bathroom, but who can have a water fight without everything and everyone getting soaked!

She came in fussing, but her grin gave her away. She took Robbie and I took Danny, dried them in big towels and put them in pajamas to be tucked into bed.

Then we both gave a big sigh. It was our time together and with any luck, it would be our quiet time. Later lying in bed, as I held my wife in my arms, we talked about our upcoming vacation time and what we would do. I didn't know that this had been the last day of my so-called normal life.

The Day My Life Was Changed Forever

Friday, July 28, 1967 began like all other days. The alarm went off at 6:30 a.m. Micki and the boys were still asleep; I leaned over, gave her a kiss and told her not to get up. I would get my own breakfast. I wasn't really all that hungry and I would see her tonight.

I looked in on our boys curled up in little balls and sleeping peacefully. I gently kissed their little heads and quietly left the room. It's funny as I look back on the day before and that morning, how happy I was. Still, I took my family and my life for granted. I had nothing more on my mind than doing a day's work and then coming home, and where we would be going on vacation the next week.

After I got to work and joined the guys on the loading dock, we discussed the changes we were going to make that day. We wanted it to go easier and quicker then yesterday.

At eight o'clock all the crew was present. Oscar Martin was talking to Francis McKee (or "Mac" as he was known to everyone), who was the head engineer of the station's department.

We went to the station's shop at the back of the headquarters building to pick up some additional work equipment. While we were getting the equipment, Oscar informed us that there were going to be some changes in our work orders for the day. He had received a call from system operator, requesting we go to Easton, Maryland substation where they had an emergency. An insulator had flashed over on an under slung dead blade disconnect.

Now let me explain what that is, since it is imperative to the story. The insulator malfunctioned and allowed the electricity to go to ground, opening the breaker and interrupting the flow of electricity to the city of Easton.

Oscar called and requested the one-and-only bucket truck in the area, only to be told it was not available. So we started toward Easton with minimal equipment, since we had planned to be in Berlin that day unloading the breakers again.

We arrived at the Easton substation between 9:00 and 9:30 a.m.

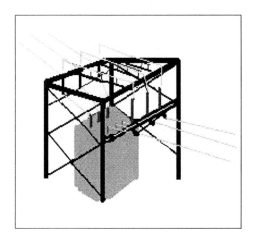

(As you can see on the drawing this is a structure made of galvanized steel about 45 feet high.) We found the porcelain insulator that had in fact flashed over, so the electric current had created a path to ground. In this case, the path was to the steel structure that was grounded.

To correct the problem, the system operator had to be contacted for switching. This was to isolate the damaged device from energized conductors. Oscar Martin called the system operator and requested switching instructions. This is a procedure that is always followed to provide maximum safety for the workers. (The system operator controls all work being done in the substations, transmission and distribution lines.)

Oscar received the switching instructions, with a designated number for this particular job. Oscar and I opened the air break switches on the 87 Y transformer structure, along with the other switch points, to isolate the area in which the flashed over insulator could be repaired.

All switches were opened and blocking tags were placed on each open switch. The red blocking tags are placed on each open switch to prevent anyone from closing them while work is being done.

After all switches were opened and tags placed, the system operator gave Oscar permission to test, ground and proceed with his work. But you must be aware that between open and tagged switches on permit number (XX. X), you must consider all other equipment energized.

Now the question was how to get a man up in the air to repair the damaged insulator. We had no bucket truck, and the two hook ladders with which we would have connected were now in Berlin. We did, however, have a 24-foot extension ladder, which we decided to take apart.

We would tie two slings (10 foot sections of rope) on one end so we could attach one end of that section to the truss (a beam on the substation). The other end would have a tag line attached from the ladder to the line truck. (The line is a 100 foot of rope used to hold different objects in a fixed position.)

After a short discussion on how we were going to complete the job, I got my body belt with tools and a hand line (a 100-foot length of rope with a pulley on the end--- the pulley being a block with two snaps and a hook. This is used by the person in the air—either on a pole or steel structure—to be able to retrieve tools and equipment from the personnel on the ground).

After getting the hand line, I proceeded to the nearest vertical I beam. Since we had no other extension ladder, I climbed the vertical I beam and cross bracing to reach the lightning arrestor truss.

The following might be a little confusing for someone who doesn't know about a substation. But I'm going to give you the facts as they are and then try to clarify them to help you understand the structure I was on and why the accident happened.

The lightning arrestor truss is a series of channel iron and angle iron pieces bolted together. This configuration forms a flat mounting surface for electrical equipment. The angle iron pieces 1.5 x 1.5 inches by approximately 36 inches are crisscrossed between 24-inch channel iron pieces, approximately 28 feet in length.

The lightning arrestor (or L. A.) truss is attached to the two vertical I beams on the backside of the structure. The three lightning arrestors (one per phase) are connected to bus tubing. This tubing is mounted on the top of the 87 Y transformer structure by means of a 4/0 copper wire or jumper the height of each lightning arrestor stack (called stack because several arrestors are bolted together forming a stack-like configuration dependent upon the voltage being protected and the number of arrestors necessary to perform the required task). For 69 KV, this required an arrestor stack of approximately 8 feet in height from the top of each LA.

The 4/0 copper jumper connects to a copper bus tubing or pipe, which is supported by insulators called bus supports. These bus or tubes extend across the top of the transformer structure to the front, and jumpers connect to the 69 KV transmission line above the gang operated air break switch.

I know all this sounds confusing and it is a little hard to comprehend. However, if you study the diagram that I have included, I hope you get a better understanding.

The key point here is the point of attachment to the transmission line. Above the open and tagged air break switch, all conductors within the structure would have been be energized.

My knowledge of this structure and its electrical continuity was very limited. I had just begun my third year of apprenticeship when I climbed the structure.

As I stood on the L.A. truss next to the left rear vertical, my thoughts and communications were with Gene Shirk, Ben Richardson and Lester Lynch. I would attach the hand line to the horizontal I beam which tied the two back vertical I beams together as well as the lightning arrestor truss. I would then request the hot stick to check the L.A. jumper for voltage. (The hot stick is a wooden pole approximately 8 feet in length and hollow, with a fiberglass wad running its length. At the end of the fiberglass rod is a brass snap/ hook, which can be opened and closed by a slide grip on the bottom end. It is sometimes called a shotgun, because the sound it makes when opened and closed is sharp.)

The next step, if the line is energized, would be to place grounds on the L.A. jumper. If the air break switch was closed accidentally, the L.A. above the dead blade under slung disconnected where I was working would then be energized. The ground would be an added step of protection.

Now to attach my hand line to the horizontal I beam above my head. The I beam was approximately 10 feet above the LA Truss and I am just under 6'2". So I could not reach the I beam while the men on the ground were assembling ropes and slings to one half of the 24-foot extension ladder.

Gene Shirk, apprentice lineman second year, was preparing his tool belt to assist me. Gene is from Princess Anne, Maryland, raised in a farming community. He is a soft-spoken, hard-working, church-going individual... the kind of person you would want on your team any day.

Ben Richardson, the journey lineman, was directing the assembly of what would be needed to complete the job. He had been a foreman for 11 years and had tremendous knowledge of the entire electrical system. Ben was in his 50s and had come up through the ranks when times were hard and so were the men. There was no such thing as a bucket truck...just hooks to climb the highest poll. The problem with Ben was that when he communicated with younger men, he treated them like second-class citizens. Several men left his crew within the 11 years, most because they felt no respect for him and disliked his inability to communicate—not because of his lack of knowledge. (I was the last one to leave his crew.) Two weeks later, he was relieved of his position of foreman and demoted to journeyman lineman. He was assigned to Oscar Martin's crew, where I had been transferred. Surprisingly this presented no problem. We communicated much better in this surrounding.

Lester Lynch, from Selbyville Delaware, was an ex-Navy man who attended the University of Delaware for three years before coming to work with the electric company. He was an even-tempered, high energy, hard-working individual ... another one of those types you would want on your team.

Landis Donaway, winch truck and heavy equipment operator, was in his 50s. A World War II veteran, he was small in stature but big and strong with heart and knowledge. (Sometimes we would get him to tell us what it was like during World War II. His experiences ranged from building the famous Burma Road to combat situations that would raise the hair on the back of your neck. And hearing the stories firsthand, you knew this man had to have been to hell and back.) Landis had a great eye for detail. By this, I mean he watched every move of every man in the air. He was constantly talking to the man in the air, no matter what their classification or experience. He was constantly keeping an eye out for whatever danger lurked in the work area.

This morning it was his turn to go for coffee. No good lineman can work all day without a good cup of coffee and I feel from the bottom of my heart that had Landis not gone to get coffee, the accident would never have happened.

Oscar Martin, in his late 50s, had been a journeyman lineman and then foreman for several years. All the men liked working for Oscar because he was easy to get along with and just a generally nice man. Ben clearly had the greater knowledge, but Oscar clearly had the most people skills.

Oscar had his own problems. He was an alcoholic. However, he had not had a drink in over 20 years. He kept his Bible with him and would preach the Gospel to anyone who would stand still long enough to listen.

Oscar was not in the immediate area when the next stage of this series of events unraveled. It is my guess that he was in the relay house, a small brick building where all the controls for breakers, re-closers and numerous switching devices are located. The telephone he was using to talk to the system operator was also located in there.

* * *

With everyone on the ground assembling the rigging, I was on the L.A. truss with my hand line. With the overhead horizontal I beam higher than I could reach, I still needed to attach the hand line to it. I took a large coil portion of the hand line in my left while taking the block and a short length of hand line in my right hand.

I threw the short length over the horizontal I beam and, as it sometimes happens, it did not go all the way over. The block lay on top of the I- beam, just out of reach. With the large coil of hand line in my left hand, I took about two loops of it to increase the length of rope for my right hand. I then whipped the rope in my right hand with the intent of getting the block and snap lose to fall across the horizontal beam where I could attach it to the beam.

The block and snap loop just slid down the beam toward the lightning arrestor. I repeated the motion and saw all the block and snap loop fall into the 4/0 copper jumper on the top of the 69 KV lightning arrester.

The next thing I remember was my vision becoming impaired. Everyone on the ground looked like a black and white photo negative. I saw Lester Lynch with his hands up over his head, apparently saying something that I could not hear.

Every muscle in my body started to spasm. I couldn't stand still. It stopped for a second and then started all over again.

I was losing my balance. I got down on my knees on the truss. I was trying to hold on and not fall to the ground. Somehow I placed my right leg through the angle iron cross bracing of the truss. At this point, I lost consciousness and fell over backwards. I hung upside down by my right leg, which was still attached to the angle iron bracing of the truss.

The next few segments of this event were later told me by members of the crew. I was hanging upside down with all my clothes on fire… pieces of burning flesh, melting steel and clothing fell to the ground. It was said that my entire body was engulfed in flames.

Gene, Ben and Lester quickly got a fire extinguisher. Gene climbed the transformer structure and sprayed me to put out the fire. He then checked me to see if I was breathing. I was not; my mouth was locked closed.

Gene told the crew on the ground I was dead. So I was hanging upside down with my clothes burned off and presumed dead.

Ben then climbed the structure. He and Gene took my hand line, which was still attached, and connected it to the overhead horizontal I beam. They attached the hook on the hand line to the day ring on my body belt, which had not burned off. (The day ring is the point of attachment on a body belt, where the safety strap—used to fasten one's self in a secure position while working with both hands—is positioned.

With a hand line attached to the d-ring of my tool belt, they dislodged my right foot and lowered me to the ground. They still assumed that I was dead. As I was being lowered, approximately 3 feet above the ground, the hook on the hand line separated from the d-ring on my body belt, and I hit the ground hard. For whatever reason, it caused my heart to start beating and my breathing to resume on its own.

I remember opening my eyes and seeing several people looking down at me. They were holding me down and telling me to lie still. I remember a black lady who lived in a house near the substation placing a blanket over me and crying while doing it. I wanted to sit upright but was held down by several men.

I had a terrible headache. I thought someone had dropped a wrench on my head. I asked what happened. Then I heard an ambulance's siren in the distance.

* * *

The personnel from the ambulance crew and line crew placed me on a stretcher and fastened me with straps. I was taken directly to Easton hospital. As soon as I was taken into the emergency room, a doctor appeared by my side. I don't remember his name, but I asked him what happened. He gave no response.

He asked me if I could sit up, which I did. He then told me to lie down. I asked for something to drink; I was so thirsty. He asked the nurse to get me some Ginger ale. I greedily drank it and asked for a second. He told the nurse it was okay, but to get a kidney tray in case I would get sick.

I drank the second one down, it tasted so good. Suddenly I felt sick. I lost both glasses quickly. I needed that kidney tray.

The doctor told me to lie down and told the nurse to cover me up with a blanket. Then he left the room for a short time.

When he returned, he told me that he had requested the ambulance drivers to transport me to Johns Hopkins hospital in Baltimore.

His next statement scared me so badly for he said, "Mr. Buck, I'm afraid I can't do anything for you."

I still didn't know what had happened, but I then knew it was serious.

I was placed back in an ambulance. Gene Shirk and a nurse got in with me. My head felt like it was going to explode.

They locked the stretcher down and closed the door. The ambulance driver must have been a stock car driver in his spare time; we were moving so fast with sirens blaring.

I lost consciousness for a while. When I woke up, there sat Gene beside me, crying. The nurse was also crying and I didn't understand why.

I asked Gene, "What happened?"

He replied that I had been in a terrible accident. When I asked what kind of accident, he said I had been electrocuted. I tried to ask how but lost consciousness again.

I found out later that the nurse was crying because my body had started to swell. This made it extremely difficult to get an IV started. She was afraid she was going to lose me even before we got to Johns Hopkins hospital.

From time to time when I became semi-conscious, the sound of the siren hurt my head so badly, and I fell into unconsciousness again, which was a blessing. I remember the sound of the siren echoing in an enclosed area or building. It was so loud; I just wanted it to stop.

I could hear many people talking and shouting commands to each other and at this point I couldn't open my eyes. I assumed we had arrived somewhere.

I remember being placed on a table; I knew people were on both sides of me and at my head and feet, also. I could hear them talking to each other calmly but constantly, and I could feel them doing different things to my body. Still I couldn't see what was happening.

I felt pin pricks at several different locations on my body. Then I knew I was being washed with soap and water or some kind of fluid. There was a distinct sound of short and intermitting buzzes like that of a bug landing on a bug lamp.

I was being turned from side to side then back to my stomach over and over. At this point I either lost consciousness or was given medication intravenously to help me relax. I don't remember what happened until I awakened in a hospital bed.

When I opened my eyes, I could see what looked like a plastic box over my head. Tubes were in my mouth and nose. I was very confused. I could see that my body was totally wrapped in bandages and I was strapped down to a bed. I could not move my arms or legs.

The nurse on duty, seeing that I was awake, asked me how I felt. I asked her to please remove the plastic box that was around my head. She gently told me that she couldn't do it. That it was an oxygen tent and it would assist me with breathing.

* * *

I still had a terrible headache, but I was now starting to feel like I was on fire. Apparently I received more medication and fell asleep. When I awoke, I opened my eyes to see my wife, Micki, standing beside my bedside. I was so glad to see her.

Our conversation was casual in content, with reference to the fact that I might be in the hospital for a few days until I got better.

She then proceeded to ask questions about the tires for our 1964 Ford Falcon Futura. We were in need of new tires and she would take care of that while I was in the hospital. She asked questions like what size and kind of tires were on the car and where she should go to purchase new ones.

She acted so calmly that it took some of my fears away. Then after a few more questions about different things at our house, she squeezed my hand and said she would be back in a little while.

I later found out that when she arrived at the hospital, Dr. Leann (the chief emergency room and critical care doctor) had told her, "Mrs. Buck, we have a very sick guy here."

When she asked, she was told I wouldn't make it through the night. She asked for odds that she could hold on to, and she was told 20%.

She asked, "Do you mean 20% that he will die?"

There was only a 20% chance that I would live. Then she was told that she could go in and see me but only if she showed no emotion… that she was to ask me questions to see if there was brain damage but again not to show any fear or emotions on her face.

I think I passed the test ... at least we have debated that fact for the next 40 years. But I honestly don't know how she did it... what an actress.

I later found out that when she left the room, the doctors grabbed her arms, thinking she was going to pass out. But she assured them that she wasn't; she was one strong lady for being so young. At the time of the accident, I was 25 and Micki was 24.

After talking to her, I thought I was only going to be in the hospital for a few days. She made me feel like it wasn't that serious and that I was going to be okay quickly. I didn't know the journey was just beginning.

For the next several months, I endure a daily ritual consisting of having bandages from head to toe changed every four hours through the day and night. A group of nurses would stand beside my bed, removing the bandages.

Then I was placed in a portable bathtub filled with warm water. I was washed from head to toe with a solution called Physohex, an antibacterial liquid. It was applied to a washcloth and two or three nurses would start scrubbing.

By this time the burning sensation was all over my body and had increased in severity. The level of burning was like that of placing a lit cigarette between your fingers and holding it there, never letting it go until it burned out.

I couldn't get away from it. I cried, screamed, prayed, and cursed all within the same breath. The nurses had to continue although they were not ignoring my pleas for them to stop; after all they were trying to save my life.

With the bathing was completed; I was lifted out of the tub and placed back on a clean bed. Then the application of a cream called sulfa- mylon, (an experimental drug that they had flown in from an Air Force base in California) was applied all over my body.

The Vietnam War was going on and the hospital at the base had received quite a few burn cases. This cream looked like cold cream with the same consistency. It was applied to all the burned areas, which was 85% of my body with a tongue depressor. They did not even want the nurses touching it with gloves on.

Once all my body was covered, I was then wrapped in bandages, only to have this process started all over again in four hours, 24 hours a day. The majority of the burns were third degree, which would require skin grafts at a later date.

The first line of attack was to keep me alive. Dealing with electrical burns is very different than say, a fire burn… although I had fire burns also when my clothes caught on fire. But an electrical burn damages the body from the inside, progressing to the surface. That is why first degree burns turn into second and second into third.

Over the next several days and weeks, the pain got progressively worse. Each day my wife would come in as soon as they allowed her and spent the whole day by my side. She would talk to me about the most normal everyday things, like what the boys were doing, the latest news back home … anything to try to keep my spirits up and not let me dwell on my injuries.

I began to notice different things with in the room. I was the only patient in the room. Above the bed was an incandescent light that stayed on all day and night. There was a window—rectangular in shape but in a horizontal position at eye level—beside the only door the room with a drawn curtain.

* * *

A doctor sat beside my bed and had been there for 3 days. He was there every time I woke up. He didn't talk except to ask me how

I felt and told me to lie still and try to relax. His left hand was always holding my right wrist. The only time he left was to get something to eat or go to the restroom.

His name was Dr. Freeman. I watched him grow a healthy beard. This was his post 24 hours a day... napping when I did. But every time I woke up, he was there. I felt very reassured.

After those five days straight, he was transferred to another patient and I never saw him again. What a dedicated young doctor. When he finished his residency, he would be one of those special young doctors who put their patients first above all. I wish I could have told him how much his being there helped me in my struggle, knowing I was never alone.

* * *

After about a week, the doctor in charge of my case changed. Dr. Leann turned my case over to the Chief Resident of Plastic Surgery, a doctor by the name of Michael Jabaley. He was a man of about 5'10" with a piercing base voice. When you heard his voice you knew who was coming, but at the same time the sound was pleasant to hear and easily understood. You could tell he had a heart of gold but was very articulate and specific in his orders for all things.

As if things were not bad enough, my wife came into the room with a handful of papers and a letter. She was very concerned with the letter, because it was my draft notice from the army. She didn't know what to do.

Dr. Jabaley looked them over and said he would take care of them. I remember thinking, *After I get out of here, I will be in Vietnam.* I asked Dr. Jabaley if he could have me well enough in time for our sixth wedding anniversary. I wanted to take my wife out for dinner somewhere special.

He asked me when that would be and Micki and I both said, "August 3rd". He said I would have to postpone that for a while.

I got very depressed, still not realizing just how seriously I was injured. He saw that I was slipping into depression and said he would do his very best to get me out of here as quick as he could. He gave instructions to my new nurse to give me a shot and soon I was drifting into a deep sleep, which lasted about 20 minutes.

* * *

The doctors frequently checked the three IV's that ran to different parts of my body. I had one in my arm, one in my groin, and one in my ankle. There were four bottles hanging from each of these polls with fluid dripping constantly.

After each bath, which was done every four hours, I would be in so much pain but exhausted at the same time that I would fall asleep for a few minutes.

After one of my naps, I awoke to find Micki in my room, although it was early. They allowed her to come in about eight a.m. every morning. Unfortunately Johns Hopkins was in a very bad neighborhood and the doctors felt it was not safe for her to walk after dark by herself, so she had to return to the hotel by five in the evening.

At that time Micki was living at the Holiday Inn, which was across the street. The union was gracious enough to make sure she had a place to live. If there was a particular bad day and she stayed after dark, one of the doctors would walk her back to the motel.

Most of the doctors' lodgings were in a building called the 550 building, which was right next door to the motel.

* * *

One morning when I woke up and looked around, I was startled. I asked Micki to come close to me and when she did, I asked her to bend down I wanted to tell her something.

When she did I whispered, *"What is that black woman doing sitting in the chair at the foot of my bed?"*

This was the 60s, before integration. So, I didn't have much contact with the black race of people. (As a small child, the only time I did have contact was a very bad experience, which left a bitter taste in my mouth. I had just gotten a new bicycle for Christmas and a group of black children had pushed me off my bike and had taken it. My mother got it back with many apologies from their parents. But it had scared me so badly that I stayed away from that part of town, which was only a half-mile away.)

When Micki told me that this was my new nurse, I thought, *Oh, God! What next! How could she know anything about nursing a burn patient? She wouldn't care if I lived or died. After all, I was white.*

Little did I know that this quiet, very professional, young Southern woman, who carried out every order given to her by Dr. Jabaley and all the residents with in his group, would come to be so important to me.

As I looked at this lady, one of the residents came in and stood beside her with his arm over her shoulder. He looked at her and said, "This is one of the best damn burn nurses and Johns Hopkins Hospital."

That was my introduction to Mrs. Clara Hammie (now Leake), or Hammie as she asked to be called, in her soft southern voice. Every morning I took comfort when she came on duty. The night nurse was good but somehow lacked her touch.

She, too, continued with the portable torture chamber, as I called it. But the gentleness and care with which she completed the necessary task made me realize she not only cared about my living but also my comfort.

The drugs I received were starting to do things to my mind and I was starting to hallucinate. I came to my senses and knew I was somewhere that seemed real, but I couldn't remember where I was. I had never been around drugs before; the strongest thing I ever smoked was a pipe full of Old Briar pipe tobacco.

Oh, I had been drunk as a kid, but this scared me. Not knowing what I was doing during those times continued to be of a great concern. When Micki came in, I asked Hammie if Micki and I could have a few minutes alone. She said sure and left the room.

I then saw what the rectangular window was for. She left the room to give us privacy but would not take her eyes off me in case something happened.

I told Micki about these hallucinatory trips I was taking... the drug-induced journeys. I was so afraid I would say something negative to Hammie during these trips and I didn't want to hurt her feelings for anything. She had become so special to Micki and me.

Micki knew of my childhood experiences and said she would take care of it. When Hammie came back into the room, Micki asked her if they could have lunch together.

Hammie said sure. As soon as it was her lunch break, both of them left. Another nurse stayed with me while Hammie was at lunch, and from time to time the floor nurse would come to the window and looked in. I couldn't do anything without somebody watching.

Micki and Hammie returned about 45 minutes later. They both came to my bedside, and Micki's smile told me everything was okay. Boy was I relieved! I had had nightmares of saying something to Hammie and hurting her.

Wow, a black woman, and I cared about her. Who would have thought! Little did I know that this was just the beginning of a family relationship that would go on even as I write this book. Sometimes even now when the phone rings and this southern voice says, "Ed," drawn out as only a Southern person can, I know right away who it is. Then after we talk for a little bit, she asks, "Is Michelle there?" (She never called her Micki— always Michelle.)

* * *

It was time for me to sit up in bed and then to get out of bed and walk from the door to a chair placed by the outside window.

The room was rectangular with a door from the hallway and a window next to it. A dresser placed under that window held medical supplies. My bed sat in the middle of the room. The wash basin had a mirror over it... two chairs... both hard back... one over head light... and a window on the outside wall overlooking more hospital roofs.

When I started getting out of bed, I noticed paper towels were taped over everything. I asked why the paper towels were all over and Hammie quickly said that it was to prevent me from coming in contact with any germs.

Even on the mirror? (I later found out that was so I couldn't see my own image in it. That would have been very depressing for me to see my face. I guess I wasn't a very pretty sight, but I didn't know my face had swollen up to the size of a basketball and it took quite a while for it to go down.)

I was sitting on the side of the bed with both bandaged feet on the floor. Two assistants, one on either side helped me, I attempted to walk the distance between the bed and window three times then sat for a bit. With the three IV poles and all the lines to tangle, this was not an easy process.

Once I was in the chair, I was supposed to eat my meals. But this was difficult and painful, since my mouth and tongue were covered with ulcers. Every mouthful of food I took was without taste and hurt the inside of my mouth so badly that I refused the food.

Hammie told me that if I didn't eat, they would be forced to put a tube back down my throat to feed me. I didn't want that. So I tried to continue eating, with tears coming out of both eyes. The additional pain on top of the constant burning pain was driving me to the edge.

I was losing weight at an alarming rate and they offered to provide me with any food I could eat. Steaks, eggs, pizza, pork— you name it and they would get it for me.

I tried so hard to eat, but everything tasted the same, and the pain it caused to try to chew and swallow almost made it impossible to tolerate. Then they tried a mixture of lactose (it looked like clear water with two raw, beaten eggs, along with a huge amount of sugar), which was so sweet it made me sick.

* * *

The first time they put a bottle of beer in my hand, I looked at them in surprise. Beer? In a hospital?

They told me that I would have to drink three bottles a day … not only to increase my appetite but to flush out the kidneys. (One of the major concerns for a severely burned patient is kidneys failure. I was to force liquids for that reason, and actually looked forward to having my beer!)

I have to laugh when I think of the young residents coming in holding a lighter under their hand and saying, "Mr. Buck, if I light this, can I be a burn patient to and have one of your beers?"

* * *

One thing that bothered me in the beginning was that the doctors—Dr. Jabaley and 10 or 12 student doctors— would come in my room every morning and early evening. All the covers would be removed, exposing my naked body. I promptly grabbed and covered myself, only to have them removed again.

They would discuss each burned area from my head to my toes; the condition of progress or lack thereof was observed by each and discussed limitedly. Only when I asked a question was there any lengthy discussion, and it was very general.

The covers were replaced and all exited the room until the next visit. After a few days of this embarrassing routine, when I saw them coming, I would throw the covers off myself, regaining some control over my situation.

I constantly asked Dr. Jabaley when I could go home. He said to give them another week or so and then we would see. Little did I know that another week or so was in reality 4 1/2 months before I left the hospital for the first time.

* * *

This next part is as hard for me to write as it will be for you to read. As bad as the baths every four hours and the reapplying of the sulfa-mylon along with changing the bandages had pushed me to the limit… then came what is called de-breeding.

One day two orderlies came with a stretcher and told me they were taking me to be do de-breeding. I asked Hammie where I was going and she replied that I was being taken to whirlpool bath called a Hubbard tank.

I asked her if she was coming and she told me only doctors would be there. It was in the physical therapy department.

The Hubbard tank is a stainless steel tank which looked to be about 3 feet deep and seven or 8 feet long.

I was transferred to a stainless steel framed canvas type stretcher. An overhead hoist was attached to this stretcher with stainless steel rods, and I was lifted and lowered into the warm water, which was also laced with Physohex. The Physohex created a burning sensation every time it was used, but it was a necessary evil.

The doctors took their scalpels and started cutting away the dead skin, but also had to cut back to live skin in order to get it all to cut down on the chances of infection. So I was in this tank with four doctors cutting, all the while seeing the water turn red with blood.

I tried to get off the stretcher and out of this damn nightmare, I couldn't stand the pain anymore. I screamed, pleading with the doctors to stop. I grabbed the stainless steel rods and actually bent them while trying to knock myself out by hitting my head on the side.

I had had enough. I couldn't stand any more. I was going mad. I was going to lose my mind.

When they stopped and took me back to my room. I literally cried on my wife's shoulder, telling her I couldn't do this anymore. When I told her what they had done, I could see the pain in her eyes.

She had known what was going to take place. Hammie had told her exactly what I was going to go through. Tears ran down her face, and we just held each other.

I looked over at Hammie and she, too, had tears in her eyes. But I was mad at her. I told her she should have told me what was going to happen.

She said it was better for me not to know. She told me I would forget this pain before long and it would be a dull nightmare.

40 years later, I still remember it as if it was yesterday. I think that's the only thing Hammie ever told me that was wrong.

* * *

Micki endured almost as much terrible pain and suffering as I. Maybe not the pain, but my God, the suffering she went through. She stood by and watched as I went from one stage of recovery to another. She saw and heard the pain and frustration I was subjected to.

Hammie showed much empathy and concern for my mental well-being as well as physical. By this time, Micki was involved in the nursing process. Hammie had decided that for her well-being, she needed to feel useful. So she taught Micki the sterile techniques and to assist in all my dressings.

Most of the time Micki has the ability to take a negative situation and bring something positive out of it. She can even get people and me to laugh at things that had been so horrible to experience but had a humorous side that only she can see. Yep, that's my Micki, my Angel sent to me from heaven! I was just beginning to see how strong and dependable she was and is. She would be the one to hold her family together and make it all work.

After Hammie and Micki went home for the evening; the night nurse came on duty at 7 PM. He and Hammie worked 12-hour shifts. (Although I had him for a while, I don't remember his name.)

* * *

As I mentioned earlier, the light in the middle of the ceiling burned 24 hours a day seven days a week. The pain would decrease with the help of both Demerol and morphine, but these drugs induced "trips". (Micki would tell me later of my "trips".)

One time I thought I was on a fishing boat and it was raining. I was worried about the people that didn't have covering on another boat. And I told her to tell them to get on our boat to they could get out of the rain.

Another time I thought I was placed on a skewer over an open fire and I could see my body parts burning and falling into the fire. I would yell out,-"Please, stop! Stop! Please, help me."

This happened both at night and during the day. The night nurse or Hammie would shake me until I woke up. Then when they asked me what was wrong, I couldn't remember. I didn't want to tell them all that I was experiencing, because I didn't think they would understand.

On one "trip" I asked Micki to remove my cigar from between my fingers of my right hand. It was burning my hand and I didn't want to catch the bed on fire. There was no cigar. Another time I was afraid someone would steal the money I had under my pillow. I was adamant there <u>was</u> money under my pillow.

Hammie and Micki raised my head and "removed" the money and told me they were taking it to the bank downstairs. When they played along, it calmed me down and enabled me to rest.

On another of my so-called *trips* I thought Taffy, our long-legged Beagle, was on the foot of my bed. I was concerned she would get tangled in the IV, pulling at the needles, so Micki picked her up and took her out of the room. Actually Taffy was with our two little boys who were living with Micki's mother and father.

* * *

One time I had had enough of the hospital. I was going home. I was on my hands and knees crawling across the bed toward the door. Hammie was desperately trying to get me on my back when we both heard the Whistler. (Dr. Richard Pipkin would always whistle as he came down the hallway.) So we opened the door.

I guess it was quite a sight for him to see Hammie and me in a struggle, I was trying to leave and she was trying to keep me from hurting myself.

He just stood in the doorway and calmly said, "Don't let him tear out my IV's."

He didn't say another word—just watched until Hammie won the battle and all was secure. Then the door closed and the whistling resumed as he continued down the hall to his next patient.

Hammie and I still laugh about this incident. We both agree I looked like something wild all tangled up in some vines. She persuaded me to be calm or she would be forced to strap me to the bed. I didn't want that—I remembered being strapped down and what it was like.

* * *

A few days later when Micki came back into the room, she brought me some munchies she thought I might eat, and told me I had company. I asked who it was and she told me it was Gene Shirk and Lester Lynch, the two who helped save my life.

I was so happy to see my buddies again. They came over to the bed and I could see from the shock on their faces that I didn't look the same. But they were kind and gentle in their conversation with me. Nothing was mentioned about my appearance or why the paper towels covered everything.

They pulled out a bag with what looked to be a watch box. I knew my watch had been burned off but wondered how I was going to wear a watch at this time with my arms all bandaged.

By this time the union had stopped paying for a hotel room. But thanks to Dr. Jabaley and his wife, Mary, Micki was now living in a small three-room apartment. It was a furnished one bedroom, living room kitchen combined and a small bathroom. But it was within walking distance to the hospital, which was so important.

We still had our little bungalow in Fruitland. The expense of paying rent and utilities there and trying to keep the apartment in Baltimore along with the telephone was more than we could handle.

Micki didn't want me to know how tight money was and how she didn't know from week to week how long she could stay there. She tried to gently tell me there was a possibility that she might have to go home soon, but I didn't want to hear that. I couldn't do it without her, I would give up.

We had no one we could ask for money, so we just had to go on faith one day at a time.

* * *

Back to my visitors, I thanked them as I took the watch box and started to talk about different things to them. But they told me to open the box.

I didn't want to hurt their feelings, so I opened it. And much to our surprise, a thick wad of bills—more money then I had ever seen at one time—fell out on my chest.

Micki and I both gasped. I looked at them and then at Micki. Tears ran down both of our faces and I just couldn't thank them enough.

To this day, we don't know how they knew how desperate we were. They told us that employees from Maryland, Delaware and Virginia had taken up a collection. There was enough in there for Micki to stay another month. I would be able to have my life line a while longer.

I noticed that Lester Lynch had his hand bandaged. I asked what happened to him. He told me he had burned his hand while removing a piece of melted steel from my chest. I felt so guilty, but thankful at the same time.

We talked for a short time and then they returned to Salisbury. I wasn't up to company for very long. I was exhausted. But this had been a really nice reprieve from my daily routine of what can only be described as torture.

* * *

The days continued with the dressing and bathing every four hours and my daily visit to the Hubbard tank for de-breeding. After the first time, Micki insisted she go with me so I would know she was right outside the door

On one particular day, the most painful one by far, all four doctors were cutting on each side from head to toe. I remember screaming from the bottom of my lungs when one of the doctors took a pair of scissors and opened them wide. He took the blade of the scissors and pushed it into the exit wound on my right foot.

The electrical current flow had been from the wet and dirty nylon hand line to the base of my left thumb. The left hand was holding the coil of my hand line. From the base of my left thumb, the current came out of my arm at the left elbow, blowing my left biceps to pieces. It then went across the shoulders, chest, head, neck and face area, then went back into the body, down both legs with the exit point being my right foot.

The right ankle bone was burned like charcoal. So after inserting the blade of the scissor into the foot, the doctor cut my foot open from my big toe to the instep of my foot. Blood ran out of my foot into the water that was already red.

I continued to scream, cry and curse in the same breath. I then heard screaming from the hallway and beating and banging on the door. Dr. Jabaley went to the door where Micki was standing sobbing, hard begging him to give me something to help the pain.

He put his arm around her and led her back down the hall, telling her he couldn't give me any more. He had, as he put it, given me enough to put down a large elephant and any more would kill me.

At this point I didn't care....*Just stop the pain... give me more... kill me... I don't care.* But there was nothing they could do; they couldn't put me to sleep, because it was impossible to put me to sleep every day; my heart wouldn't take it. The cutting was necessary to keep the wounds as clean as possible, because bacteria would breed in the burned skin, so it had to be removed to keep me alive.

The down side was also the point that there were no curtains blocking my view of the cuttings, so I could virtually see my body being cut to shreds. (Curtains came after I left.) In 1967 it was so rare for a person to be as badly burned as I was and still live past a few hours.

Micki later told me that a man in the next room, to whom she spoke every day and who was not burned as badly as I, had died after five days. So she had that fear to live with.

We returned to my room, Halsted 217, Micki by my side all the way. Once back in the room I was transferred from the gurney into the bed, where the sulfa mylon and total bandage replacement continued.

The pain was so bad I screamed whenever the bandages were changed on my feet. I was so weak by this time it was difficult for me to hold up my head.

Hammie got a pair of angle glasses with mirrors on them so I could lie on my back and watch television. This was another attempt to keep my mind off the pain.

We would watch cartoons on the weekend, and I so look forward to that. There was no de-breeding done on the weekends, so that I had a reprieve. I remember watching the coyote and the roadrunner and that the coyote reminded me of myself, always a day late or a dollar short. At least the room did have some laughter and it.

* * *

When Hammie changed the bandages on my face and head, I could feel something hanging on the right side of my head and neck. I asked her what it was and she said it was just a little piece of skin. After a few days I asked if she could do something about it. She asked me if it hurt and I said no.

I didn't feel anything when she removed it and later I found out it had been my right ear. It had been burned beyond repair.

At this time I was losing amino acid from my wounds, which is another worry about a burn patient. The blood I had lost from both the accident and de-breeding was being replaced by blood transfusion—by this time I had received 26 pints. Now they had to do something about repairing the burn areas where I was losing amino acid. So it was a trip by gurney to the operating room where three doctors used a device on me that looked like a cheese cutter, a fine wire stretched between a horse-shoe shaped piece of stainless steel. This procedure is called skin grafting, where skin is taken from an area called a donor sight onion paper thin and placed over the wound; with good luck it would adhere and grow to be healthy skin.

There was minor pain with this procedure, but this was necessary to stop the loss of amino acid. Amino acid is an essential protein required to sustain life. The human body will die without a certain amount. When I returned to my room, I looked like a piece of chopped liver with more dressings to change.

Dr. Jabaley and his family took a trip to Williamsburg Virginia. The night after he left, a young doctor who had assisted in the de-breeding process came into my room. He told me he was going to give me a tetanus shot, even though the other doctors didn't want to. He said I already had enough problems and did not need to add lockjaw to them. He then gave me the shot in my left thigh. I had been asked within a few days of the accident when I had last received a tetanus shot, but I could not remember.

I don't know this doctor's name, but that was the only time I ever saw him. I only remember his being hyper about what he was doing.

A few hours later during the four-hour bath and bandage routine, I noticed that during the process removing and replacing the bandages on my feet, I had very little pain. I remember thinking, *Thank God, now maybe I can get some sleep.*

The next morning it was time to get out of bed and walk across the room before breakfast. Hammie told me to get out of bed and do my exercises while she put clean linen on the bed.

When I sat up, I noticed my feet didn't feel right; they felt numb. I told Hammie and the two orderlies (who were there to assist me with walking, because I was so weak) about my feelings. She said to stand up and try walking, which I did, and promptly fell in a heap to the floor.

The two orderlies quickly grabbed me and put me back in bed. Hammie told me to try again and when I did, I started to fall again. The two orderlies caught me and placed on the bed.

Hammie looked alarmed as she left the room, telling the two orderlies to stay with me. She was calling a doctor.

* * *

For the next couple of days, hell got worse. The doctors came in, several of them, and started asking all kinds of questions. Some of them started sticking me with pins and asking if it hurt... could I feel it?

I was terribly confused as to what was going on and why my legs would no longer support me. Then to my horror the numbness started going up my body. Ever so slowly it rose.

The doctors stuck me with pins. Where I could feel them they would make a mark on my body. By the third day the level had reached my lower abdominal area.

Now another form of torture began=like a ball of fire in my stomach. I could feel it expanding to the point where I thought it would burst. It kept coming higher.

My breathing was now affected. I was gasping for air. I couldn't stop gasping.

I continued to cry out in terrible pain. The doctors were called, but they could only stand there and monitor the process. My heart was racing.

They wanted to give me a shot of digitalis but couldn't because of my rapid heartbeat. Digitalis is a medication used to stabilize or maintain the frequency of the heartbeat. It is usually given when the heartbeat is between 80 and hundred beats per minute. But mine was 140, so that was out of the question.

They tried to get me to control my breathing to prevent hyperventilating. As hard as I tried, I couldn't stop gasping for air. A couple of the doctors had to leave; they finally couldn't stand hearing me gasping for breath—seeing the pain and not being able to do anything about it

Hammie and Micki tried their best to get me to calm down. This went on for several hours into the night. Finally late in the evening, the labored heavy breathing subsided.

By the next morning my heart rate was below a hundred beats per minute. So I was given digitalis and remained on it for several months.

By this time I lay in bed and could no longer sit up. The doctors again started with the pins and asked when I felt this. I answered no to the majority of their questions.

They drew a line across my chest just below the nipples. They said this was a level T-6, which meant nothing to me at the time. I just knew the pain from that line down was gone, although there was still plenty of pain left.

Hammie and Micki, God love their souls, could not have done more for me. They watched and listened to my every crying breath of pain, not knowing if I was going to live or die. Quite frankly, at this point I was beginning to wonder myself.

* * *

The next day Dr. Jabaley returned from his trip. He came to the side of my bed and stroked my forehead. With his melodious low voice, he asked, "What happened? You were doing so well when I left."

As he looked at my chart, I saw the frustration and anger on his face and also heard it in his voice. He also pulled out a pin and started checking all the areas on my body, asking where I could feel to find out the level.

After a few minutes he talked with Hammie and left the room noticeably upset with the condition he found me upon his return. My thoughts went back to that tetanus shot and I wondered if that was the cause of the paralysis. I wasn't paralyzed until after that shot.

The next day Hammie and an orderly placed me on a gurney and headed toward radiology. When we arrived they started taking x-rays of my body, including the *Mylogram.*

They turned me on my side and told me not to move and to hold my breath while the needle was placed in my spine. During the x-ray procedure, one technician looked at the other and said it was dead and should be taken off. I did not know what he was talking about.

I immediately became concerned and asked Hammie what he was saying. She said he was just an x-ray tech and Dr. Jabaley would make any decisions as to what was going to be done.

I didn't know they were talking about my right foot. I knew it was in bad condition. I just did not know how badly it was injured.

We left radiology and returned to Halsted 217. The doctors were still unable to figure out what had caused the paralysis, and the questions and battery of tests continued for the next several days.

Lying in my bed, paralyzed from my chest to my feet, I asked myself what was next. The answer came too quickly.

The swelling was becoming worse in my arms and legs. The swelling in burn patients can continue for weeks but now had reached the stage where I no longer had any pulse in my left hand or left foot.

Dr. Jabaley and several other doctors came in to witness this condition. They discussed various different solutions, thinking I couldn't hear them. I got sick to my stomach when I heard the suggestion to amputate both my left arm and left leg.

Then I heard Dr. Jabaley speak up and say he wanted to try something else first. All the doctors left the room, except Dr. Jabaley and a Dr. William Iams. Dr. Iams was Dr. Jabaley's right arm at that time; he accompanied Dr. Jabaley with all the different procedures. (Micki would later tell me she called Dr. Iams her pessimistic doctor. He tried to prepare her for all the pitfalls that might and probably would be encountered.) But he was straightforward and honest, a trait which I admire and would prefer.

Dr. Jabaley talked to Hammie and requested some medical equipment. When it came, he placed the equipment on a tray beside my bed. He told me he was going to perform a faciotomy. This procedure would involve cutting open my left arm from the inside of my elbow to my wrist, which in turn would relieve the pressure from the swelling – or edema, as it is called.

At this point I was willing to try anything. I didn't want to lose my arm and leg.

Dr. Jabaley started cutting as I lay there and watched. The skin snapped with a crackling sound as he slowly moved down my arm.

The muscles, veins and tendons were clearly visible. I watched the blood flowing through my veins. From time to time I could see tiny air bubbles in my veins and thought I would die when they reached my heart. It was explained to me, much to great relief, that this was the process of carrying oxygen throughout my body.

This same procedure was completed on my left leg. I endured only minor pain.

After a few minutes of cutting, Dr. Jabaley said that it worked. The pulse returned to both my arm and leg.

I could see the relief on Dr. Jabaley's face, but his next remark made me realize we were not out of the woods yet, so to speak. He said we would have to see how things went for the next few days before we took the next step.

I asked Dr. Jabaley if he was going to stitch the open wounds closed after the swelling was gone. He asked if I remembered the skin that had been taken from the various donor sites; these would be placed on the open area that, in time, will grow closed. This however, would take some time for the edema to go away and prepare the skin for the placement of the skin grafts, along with all the other areas of third degree burns that would have to be grafted. All we could do was wait and keep the infection under control.

* * *

It was now the end of August. Hammie was taking some days off. She had worked 12 hours a day, seven days a week, for several weeks now and she was burned out. She needed to recharge her body. She was going to Greensboro, North Carolina for a family reunion but would be back soon.

She could see the fear in my eyes; I so depended on her for everything and didn't want anyone else to take her place. My trust in her was total.

She tried to comfort me by telling me the nurse replacing her was very good. Then she laughingly told me that the nurse was also black so I wouldn't notice a difference. That's my Hammie!

She told me the new nurse's name, but I can't remember it now. She was very nice but also quiet—not at all as happy and talkative as our Hammie.

A couple of days later, I spiked a fever. I was placed on what was called a hypothermia mattress. This is a mattress that has air circulating through it. There is a thermometer placed in the body and attached to the mattress. This device helps regulate the body's temperature.

I did not like hearing the compressor when it inflated and circulated the air through the mattress, but this device also helps promote blood circulation and reduced the chances of decubitis ulcers or bed sores.

I remember going to sleep and feeling very warm, and I could hear the nurse talking to me but could not respond. She kept telling me to wake up over and over, but I couldn't open my eyes. I wanted to but couldn't.

I heard the door slam as she left the room and I was still unable to move. I just felt very warm and without any pain.

Then I heard the public address system in the hallway. I remember hearing a number 555 and some colors and then Halsted 217.

The next thing I heard was the nurse returning, followed by Dr.Jabaley and Dr. Iams. They talked with the nurse and got the details of what happened.

Dr. Jabeley came to my bedside and said if I could hear him, this was what he was going to do. He told me he was going to give me a shot of adrenaline in my heart. He said I would feel a pin prick and a burn. My heart rate would increase but it was nothing to worry about; I would be alright.

I felt his open hand gently slapping the side of my face while saying to wake up. I opened my eyes and he then told me that gangrene was now present in my right foot and it would have to come off.

Micki had gone to the store to get some things she needed and Dr. Jabaley met her in the hall, explaining what had happened and what was going to happen. (She later told me that she saw him come out of my room covered in blood; however he had just come out of the operating room, so the blood was not mine.) But she had been told they had almost lost me; I had gone into a coma. Then she was told she would have to sign the papers to give them permission to amputate my right foot.

I remember her standing at the foot of my bed rubbing my foot and crying. I don't know what she was thinking, not saying a word, but I could see she was hurting.

After the papers were signed, I was again transferred to a gurney and taken to the operating room. I looked back to see Micki standing in the doorway in tears as Dr. Jabaley and Dr. Iams pushed me down the hallway toward the elevator.

In the operating room, Dr. Jabaley told me he was going to put me to sleep. The next thing I remember was Dr. Iams gently slapping my face telling me to wake up.

I opened my eyes. It was all over. My right foot was gone.

We returned to my room and Micki was waiting; I could still see traces of tears on her face. All she could do was stand at the foot of the bed and rub my leg. My foot was no longer there and the crying could not be stopped.

All the memories that we had of my high school days playing football were recounted. I could hear Coach Hanley saying, "Dig, Dig, Dig, all right! Keep going and work harder" were distant memories of football practice...Coach Georgiana telling me when I had a minor injury, "You have to learn to play hurt." These two great men told me and the entire team, "You will learn more about life from football than any other sport."

Truer words have never been spoken.

For the next several months, these memories kept me trying to do my best through the existing and future challenges. The next few days were extremely difficult to adjust to—the phantom sensation, the pulse-like feeling ran down my leg into my foot which was no longer there. It felt like my foot and leg were jumping all over the bed. Actually nothing was moving; it just felt like that and it worked on my mind.

I thought this was a sign that the paralysis was leaving and all would be normal. After all, one of the nurses' aids told me that paralysis was God's way to keep me from having all that pain. I could not believe the paralysis was going to remain.

I began talking positive about when it would leave and what I was going to do. I wanted to go back to work with the prosthesis. Then we were going to get a motorcycle and would be riding through the backcountry with the cool breeze in our faces...my girl and me riding into the sunset.

Hammie and Micki listened to my ideas and were very patient for a while and let me ramble.

Then came the day when Dr. Iams walked into my room with a serious but sympathetic look on his face. He sat down by my bed and told me we had to have a talk about my future. That was okay by me. Then he said he meant long-term future.

I asked him what he had in mind. He replied he meant the possibility of the paralysis leaving was getting smaller and smaller. It was probable that I would be in a wheelchair for the rest of my life.

I let it sink in... I think I knew in my heart that this was going to be a fact. I had dealt with it. And although I did not want to admit it, I knew I had to face it.

I looked at him and told him I would be the best and fastest man in a wheelchair he had ever seen. Memories of my football coaches... put your best game on the field and everything will fall into place. You may not win the game, but you will be proud of your accomplishments.

I knew at this time this was the attitude I had to have. There was no other choice. I wanted to be as good as I could be in whatever I did in life.

Dr. Iams and I talked for a long time about different goals and options on how to achieve these goals. He squeezed my arm and told me I'd be okay... I was going to make it. And then he left the room.

Now I had to tell Micki the bad news and at the same time let her know I was not going to give up. She in turn let me know giving up was not an option.

Through the next several years I would find out just how serious she was. Every day, all day, she and Hammie pushed and probed me to do better. To be honest, at this time I did not like either one of them much.

The days passed and I was now on what is known as a circle electric bed... lying face down, both arms on IV boards shoved under the mattress pad. My forehead rested on a head support pad as I looked straight down at the floor below.

I remained in this position for several weeks. Yes, weeks—not days. This was necessary, due to donor sites on my back and hip area. Skin had been removed from these areas to be placed on the third degree burns on my face, neck, arms and legs as well as the groin area.

I was able to lie there and watch the blood travel through my veins hour after hour. My neck began to feel like it was broken. Physical therapy was now out of the question. My left arm lay in a fixed position about half way from my mouth to being straight. It would remain like this for weeks.

When I was first placed in this position, Hammie or Micki would feed me. As time went on I saw their true colors.... they were just plain mean. They told me to feed myself. I told them I couldn't; "I only have one arm that moves and I'm lying on my stomach."

But they placed a bowl of oatmeal on a low table and put a spoon in my good hand. I dropped the spoon because my hand and arm was too weak.

They picked up the spoon, wiped it off and put it back in my hand. Now – I was angry and the cussing began. Both the hand and that damn spoon were shaking like a leaf. I finally got the spoon in the oatmeal and started its upward journey to my mouth.

Hell, now it gets worse. The damn spoon shook so badly it was empty when I got it to my mouth. Now I was really angry and I wanted to fight. I - cried like a baby which only made me madder. I was shaking like a leaf and making little progress.

Later Micki told me how hard it was for her to do this. But Hammie said I had to do it for myself. I had to rely on myself and not other people or I would be weak forever.

But by this time I was just plain mad. I ate that damn oatmeal… or what made it to my mouth and not the floor.

* * *

And now let me introduce Dr. Anthony Reading or Tony Reading, as he was called. Dr. Reading sat in a chair located in one corner of my room. He arrived within the first few weeks of my hospital stay, introduced himself, and then seated himself in a chair which he would occupy every day for short period of time. He would just sit there with his pad of paper and pencil, not asking any questions, just jotting things down (like when I was in excruciating pain or experiencing anger or frustration).

Whenever I would ask him a question, he would always reply, "And what do you think?"

The days continued to go by while I lay face down on the circle electric bed. Pressure sores formed on both my knees. The doctor placed doughnut-shaped pads on my knees to relieve the pressure due to the immobility.

There was little that could be done. I remained on my stomach while the donor sites healed, the edema subsided and the graft areas were prepared to receive the new skin.

It would have been so easy for me to give up during this time, but Hammie and Micki took turns at aggravating the hell out of me. They would continually move my food just out of my reach to make me move as much as possible and develop the stamina to continue until the goal was reached.

I filled my bowl of cereal and plate of food with tears. It was so frustrating to try to feed myself while lying on my stomach suspended in mid-air with only one hand.

I tried to balance the solid food or soup on a spoon or fork while the skin and scar tissue was ripping. There were areas of third and second degree burns on my right arm, shoulder and armpit. Each time I moved that portion of the burned area, it would rip open. This routine happened daily...rip open, then heals... rip open, then heals… over and over again. Although it was painful, this process had to continue. (Therein lays the reason for moving the plate and bowls of food just out of my reach.)

During this time my left arm remained in a fixed position. While in this position, the bone chips in my elbow solidified. There is no longer an elbow joint, just solid bone. My hand and wrist were functional, but the elbow would not move. (This problem, Dr. Jabaley said, would be addressed later.) The bone chips were formed when the electrical current came down the wet and dirty nylon rope and into my left hand. The electrical current made the muscles in my left arm contract with such force that pieces of bone were removed from their point of attachment. These bone chips and calcium deposits formed a solid elbow joint.

The weeks and now months dragged on. I kept asking Dr. Jabaley if I could go home. I liked the people in the hospital but hated the hospital itself.

He told me to give him another week or two. I didn't know I was still on the critical list. I had not returned to a conventional hospital bed.

The wet-to-dry dressings now began. This was preparation for skin grafting. The swelling/edema had to be gone and the area prepared to receive the skin. (The wet-to-dry dressing is sterile gauze pads saturated with saline solution.) When the gauze was dry, it stuck to the dead skin and did a mini de-breeding although not as painful. This was done over and over until the area was clean and ready for the skin grafting.

When the gauze was pulled off, the area would bleed. My body looked like chopped liver. When the new skin was applied, it was carefully positioned with Q-tips™. The doctors would take Q-tips™ and roll them across the newly placed skin, removing any air pocket or bubble.

While Dr. Jerry Dorman, was doing the skin grafts, I asked, "How can you work on a live human body with all that blood?"

He stopped for a second, looked me in the eye, and said, "If I didn't think it would be saving your life, I couldn't."

I said no more.

Dr. Dorman continued with the grafting for that day. When completed, he placed over me an aluminum canopy that covered me from head to foot; he then attached an incandescent light bulb to the canopy and turned it on. Next he placed a bed sheet over the canopy.

I was to lie perfectly still on my back for days. The canopy with the light on kept my body warm. There was to be no contact of any material to the newly placed skin.

This is the first time being paralyzed helped. I could not move my legs if I had wanted to. But now there was a price to pay for lying on my back. You see, when the new skin grafts on my face, neck, arms chest and legs were healing, the lower portion of my spine was breaking down. The coccyxes or lower element of the backbone was now coming through the skin. The entire sacral area was becoming one large decubitis ulcer.

Surgery was necessary to remove the unneeded bones in this area. During the next few weeks, there were several trips to the operating room for skin grafts. Each time I returned to my room looking like chopped liver and wondering when it would ever end.

It was now October and I had received several visits from family and friends. The one I remember most was when Micki brought our two little boys to see me. Danny was five years old and Robbie, two years old. They were both dressed like little men in their suits.

God, it was good to see them again. I wanted to jump out of bed, pick them up and hug them so badly, but I could not move. Since I was paralyzed, I could only look at them and talk to them.

I saw fear and concern a little faces. I tried to smile and put them at ease. Micki couldn't bring them in to see me before this because we were afraid they would be too traumatized seeing me like a zombie in bandages covered with cream and my body so swollen. Now I was looking more human although not like the daddy they had last seen.

As with most kids, after a few minutes they accept things and were more at ease. We teased them and soon they were laughing with us.

I felt the best that day that I had in months. I got to see my boys. And it would be two and a half months before I got to see them again.

The boys were staying in Baltimore with Micki and my mother, Mary Buck, but there were problems, so Micki took them to Ocean View, Delaware to stay with her parents, Myron and Ella Mezick.

The time had come for surgery to repair the lower back area. There I returned to the operating room and was placed on my stomach again. I was face down the operating table when Dr. Jabaley introduced me to Dr. Rick Hansin, a well known plastic surgeon. There was also a very sweet sounding and gentle nurse present.

Dr. Jabaley explained that this operation would be completed under local anesthetic. I still had multiple IV's and would be given medication to keep me calm.

The surgery began. I heard all the comments that were exchanged. I started to become concerned when I heard statements like, "Give me a saw" or "Get me a rake, a hoe". I started to get nervous and Dr. Jabaley told the nurse to give me some Demerol to calm me down. She did and I was soon willing to get back in there and get this show on the road. I felt so good!!!

I knew a little bit about farming, having been raised in farm country. I knew how to use these instruments. They soon had me laughing when I heard my two doctors talking about subjects like outdoor sports, college subjects and—oh yes—panty raids. (Yes, we men will talk about anything, even under adverse conditions.)

As the nurse gently rubbed my arm and kept talking to me to keep my mind off the surgery; I wanted to hear more about those panty raids. She laughed and insisted I listen to her. After all, she said she was the one who was most likely telling the truth; the other stuff I was hearing was just dreams. The doctors were just saying all that stuff to get my mind off reality. Okay, if that was her story. Fine, let her stick to it.

When the surgery was completed, I returned to Halsted 217 even though I sure would love to have heard more about those panty raids from my very professional doctors.

The next few weeks involved more skin grafts and then Dr. Tony Reading spoke to me. Wow, the man could talk! He asked, "Are you willing to have a mass interview in the Phipps building?"

" What is a mass interview?" I asked. *What was a mass interview?*

He explained, "Your bed will be taken to an amphitheater, which will be filled with doctors. They will each take turns asking you questions.

Now I was concerned. "What kind of questions?"

He noticed my agitation and consoled, "It will be alright, Ed. You don't have to answer any questions that make you uncomfortable."

I agreed to do the interview.

Three days later, Dr. Reading escorted me to the stage area where I lay on my bed and looked into the faces of a hundred doctors.

He then asked that the doctors begin their questions. Boy did they ever! They asked questions about my faith in God, my mental thoughts before and during my hospital stay. They wanted my opinion on a variety of subjects, some of which would make any man blush. They left nothing uncovered.

It got to the point where I was embarrassed at both the questions and my answers. This went on for what seemed hours.

Dr. Reading saw that I was exhausted and suggested we complete the questions immediately. When it was over, they knew more about me than I did.

Back in my room, I asked Dr Reading if I was crazy.

He responded with his usual, "What do you think?"

Now I could feel fear after all I had been through. And to think for a second I may have lost my mind process was frightening.

When Dr. Reading left my room, my mind raced. *What can I do to find out if I am in fact crazy?* I was serious *Have I lost my mind because of the pain?*

The more I thought about it the worse it became.

* * *

Jenny Minchel was my physical therapist. She was a beautiful English lady with a heart of gold. She was one who really cared about all her patients.

I told Miss Minchel what had happened and how worried I was. She told me not to worry. She would have a talk with Dr. Reading.

The next day Dr. Reading arrived and told me he understood I had some concerns. I bluntly asked him if he thought I was crazy. He again asked," What do you think?" and paused for my answer.

I thought hard for a minute, looked him and said, "No. With all I have been through, I think I'm okay."

"Well that sounds fine to me," he said. "Yesterday wasn't to test your sanity, it was to help us learn about the kind of mental stress you have been subjected to and how you have been able to handle it. You have been a big help for us to understand and respond correctly to others whom we might find in the same situation. The extent of your injuries was greater than we had ever seen. So to be able to interact with you, we have learned a great deal. But you do realize you're not out of the woods yet."

"What does that mean?" I asked.

He responded, "What do you think?"

"Ah, I guess I'm not ready to go home yet."

Dr. Reading looked down at me, smiled, and left the room.

Miss Minchel, Hammie and Micki all gathered around my bed to discuss the events of the last two days. The mood shifted from tears to laughter. After a long discussion of the subjects that were covered in the interview/interrogation, we decided Dr. Reading needed to get a life. He had been confined to my room with nothing but a pad of paper and a pencil for too long. It was starting to wear on his nerves. We decided he needed to smoke a pipe or cigar, have a large glass of whiskey with a wild woman to sit on his lap.

The day ended with all of us laughing until happy tears came. Thank You, Dr. Reading!

I had so hoped to be home for Thanksgiving. Dr. Jabaley had tried hard to make it possible. But the decubitis also on my coccyx or tailbone had to be repaired by taking the bone out. So that meant the hospital stay was not over.

After several changes back and forth between the conventional bed and the circle electric bed then the removal of the coccyx's bone, I was ready for flap surgery. This was where Dr. Jabeley and Dr. Hanson surgically closed the open area where the bone had been removed.

This time things were a little different in the operating room. At least they used different yard tools. I didn't hear about a rake or a hoe. And soon it was over and I was back in my room.

The days were getting shorter. I felt the change of seasons as I looked out my window and knew winter was just around the corner.

I could now sit in a wheelchair, but I remembered the first time I tried sitting up in a wheelchair after several weeks in bed. Dr. Jabaley told Hammie he wanted me out of bed and sitting in a chair.

Two orderlies placed me in the chair by the window. I was supposed to sit there for 15 minutes. However, I passed out within five and was placed back in bed.

This procedure continued until I could sit up long enough to eat my meals. Even though I argued with Dr. Jabeley and told him I really could not do it, he turned a deaf ear to my pleading and left orders that I would get up, I would sit in a chair every day, and I would eat my meals sitting up.

Thank you, Dr. Jabaley, for making me take another step forward.

After about a week or so, I was able to sit up in a wheelchair for a good period of time. This enabled Micki to take me out of the room and off the floor.

I was getting so tired of having needles every day. Sometimes three or four times a day they would draw blood. One day as Micki and I were at the elevator getting ready to go down to the cafeteria, the door opened and a phlebotomist came out, looked at me and asked me if I was Mr. Buck. I knew what she had in mind another needle.

I very politely said, "No, he is in Halsted 217, right down the hallway."

Then I quickly got on the elevator and told Micki to come with me, because we were leaving. We laughed the whole way down stairs.

I wonder what she thought when she later found out that I was the guy she was looking for.

Going to the cafeteria and having a sandwich and watching the other people made me more human again. Doctors and nurses who had become our friends would stop by the table; sit down to talk for a few minutes. That did more to boost my spirits than about anything.

* * *

Thanksgiving was approaching. At one time we thought we might be home for that. Instead, the hospital set up a tray for Micki and we had our Thanksgiving dinner together in my room.

I was progressing and the day came when they said I would no longer be in a private room. I would be transferred to a ward and that frightened me greatly. That meant I would no longer have Hammie as my nurse.

How could I get along without Hammie? I was so used to looking up and seeing her smiling face and knowing that no matter what I needed, she would take care of me. And now I would just be another patient being taken care of by different nurses.

That should have made me happy to know that I was that much better, but it didn't. I was just afraid to be left on my own.

In a few days, Dr. Jabeley came into the ward and told me he was going to remove the last IV. If everything went well; we would be going home for Christmas, with the understanding that I would need to return to the hospital in January for more surgery.

This was the greatest news I had heard. He said they would start making plans for my discharge on December 16, 1967.

After he left the room Micki and I cried with happiness. This must mean I was finally off the critical list and out of the woods. This meant I was going to live. Thank God!

This had been a rough road, but we had made it this far. And Micki let me know we were going to make a lot farther and she would be with me all the way, no matter how tough it got.

Guess I got that one in a million.

The weather was now cold and snow was forecast.. Micki packed all her belongings from the apartment and took our car home so that she could ride in the ambulance with me. It seemed strange for her to be gone over night. She had been by my side every day except two times throughout this whole ordeal from July to December.

The next day I was worried. She had gone the day before and should have been back by then. This was in the days long before cell phones. Finally in the late afternoon she came in looking very tired. I asked her what time she left Fruitland.

She told me, "8 a.m."

It was 5 p.m. Her trip should have taken 2 1/2 hours but it had taken eight hours because of a big snow storm. She had ridden on a bus all day and when she got to the bus terminal, she had a difficult time trying to get a cab. So she looked like a wet snowman.

A few days later the big day came. It was bittersweet— so many friends to say goodbye to, the excitement of going home and being able see our little boys. Yet I had the fear of not having doctors and nurses going out of my room all day and night. That had been my security blanket.

Hammie and her husband, David, came to see us off. We were all crying. She had been such a big part of my seeing this day. I owed her my life. The bond we formed in that hospital, which she claimed she was not going to do, was there for the rest of our lives. She had gotten close to one other patient years ago and put her heart and soul in that case, only to lose him after a long period of time. It hurt her so badly she swore she would never get close to a patient again.

She was wrong.

* * *

As I was being loaded into the ambulance, Dr. Jabeley gave Micki some last minute instructions on what to do IF. Then he took my hand and squeezed it firmly. It was almost as if I could read his mind. I saw tears in his eyes and knew his heart was hurting, for he wanted me to have been able to walk out of hospital so badly.

There was such a love-hate relationship on my part. He made me do things I didn't want to do, and yet I loved that man like a big brother. He had never gotten over my becoming paralyzed. He blamed himself for not being there to oversee every move. As hard as this man was on me and how mad I got at him during the struggle of surviving, I had a hard time leaving his care even for a short period. He was my lifeline.

Micki and I was so excited and yet nervous about going home. We knew we were more or less on our own and suddenly felt like children unsure of the future—not knowing if we could handle this time on our own by ourselves.

The ambulance drivers were great. They joked and soon had us laughing.

As we were riding away from the hospital, we realized that it was one o'clock and we were hungry. I was too excited to eat any breakfast, so we stopped at a McDonald's for lunch. The driver and attendant went inside and brought us out some food.

As we sat in ambulance eating our hamburgers, people walked by the ambulance and looked into the window. Maybe they thought this was my last supper. Micki said we could do a commercial for McDonald's: *no matter your condition a McDonald's burger will fix you up!*

We found the smallest things to laugh at.

On the way home, Micki and I started making plans. Although we were not hungry now, we knew we would be by dinnertime. She laughed and told me she looked in the refrigerator when she was home and knew she had one pack of pork chops in the freezer but that was all.

Our wonderful neighbors, headed by Peggy and Bob Tarr and Jean Pope, had taken care of our little house. It was so hot that summer and since the house was closed up, humidity had taken its toll. They had gotten a humidifier and ran it 24/7 to extract gallons of water from the furniture and rugs. Then they had cleaned out the refrigerator and it was now spotless.

A ramp had been built and a hospital bed set up in the living room for me.

Once I was settled, Micki could go the store very quickly. I had not been by myself since before the accident and was a little apprehensive.

Micki's parents were bringing our boys home the next day so that we could first get settled in. I couldn't wait to see them. I missed my guys so much my heart hurt, physically hurt. But the excitement of coming home was overwhelming.

Micki said maybe she could ask Peggy or Jeanie to stay with me while she went to the store. We were both scared to leave me alone.

We were moving quickly... Southwest on US Route 50, through Easton, and that gave me a funny feeling. The last time I been here I was dying... through Cambridge, Lindwood, Vienna, and into Wicomico County.

We passed through Mardela,I knew Hebron was next and then Salisbury, where we would turn onto route 13 and head south to the greatest little town on the Eastern shore... Fruitland, Maryland.

As we traveled along route 13, I told Micki as I looked out the window the ambulance that so many things look different from what I remembered. But it all looked so beautiful.

We turned off route 13 onto Hayward Avenue. Then the ambulance pulled up in front of our house.

Micki said, "Oh My God! Look Eddie!"

I tried to sit up and saw a banner hanging from the trees in front of our house. It read, *Yup, Ed, this is it... Home Sweet Home!* Another one read, *Welcome Home!*

The yard was filled with our neighbors cheering. Of course I cried. Tears ran down Micki's cheeks, too.

We had the greatest neighbors in the world—Peggy and Bob Tarr and their daughter, Lisa; Jeanie Pope, and her three children; Tom, Linda, and Joanne; Angie and Gill Heath, with their son Russell; an older couple who lived across the street, Mr. and Mrs. Topfer. They were all there. (Mr. and Mrs. Topfer used to sit on their porch and laugh when Micki and I would play with Danny and Robbie in the backyard. I would pick her up by her feet, holding her behind my back and user her like I was lifting weights. She would squeal and beat me on my back laughing and laughing, the boys holding on to each leg. This made the older couple laugh.)

Thank God, I have those memories. It must have been a sight to watch as I was transferred from the ambulance into the house, waving to everyone with a smile on my face that would not quit while tears ran down both of my cheeks.

God, I was glad to be home. The banners, the signs, and all the people made me appreciate being alive. In spite of everything that had happened, it was all worth the fight.

We continued into the house and I was placed in the brand-new hospital bed. As I wrote previously, we lived in a little bungalow and the bedroom was not big enough for our bed and a hospital bed to boot.

From my bed in the living room, I could see all the whole downstairs—the dining room and into the kitchen. I looked at the dining room table, which was laden with food—so much food you could not see the top of the table.

Then Jeanie or Peggy (I'm not sure which one) told Micki to go into the kitchen for napkins that they had forgotten to put on the table. As she walked toward the kitchen, I saw them wink at each other and then I heard Micki gasp,-and respond with her favorite saying of the day, "Oh My God"

She came back to my bed with a shocker expression on her face. She told me that every cupboard in the kitchen was full of food... that you couldn't get a toothpick in them.

Then they told her to get some butter and when she opened the refrigerator, it was full, too. It seemed they had had what was called a pantry party. They had gone from house to house collecting money to fill our house with food, and our generous neighbors had dug deep into their pockets. Although we were all in the same boat, raising children and living pay check to pay check—except for the Topfers who were on a fixed income, everyone had contributed.

We asked the ambulance crew to join us for dinner as there was enough food to feed the entire neighborhood and more. So they stayed.

While everyone ate, there was a knock on the back door. A fellow employee, Bill Shockley, who was also a good friend and owned a grocery store, had been given money by the employees of Delmarva Power to buy us groceries. And in he came with seven boxes full of food. We could only stare, thank him from the bottom of our hearts and, of course, cry.

After everyone had gone home, we started adjusting to our return. Now exhausted after one of the greatest days in my life, I finally got to sleep in a bed in my home. Home Sweet Home!

* * *

The next day brought the greatest visitors—Micki's mother and father bringing home our little men. They had grown so much and to have them climb on my bed and give me hugs was the greatest day of all. Finally my little family was together again. Hearing their little feet running all over the place and making all kinds of normal childhood noises was just what the doctor ordered.

Even though they didn't understand why their daddy always stayed in bed, they seemed to adjust rather well and were satisfied to make periodic checks on me to make sure I was still there. They had to tell me what everyone was doing in the neighborhood while also telling on each other. It had been so long since I had experienced normal.

We had visitors from three states for the next few days—Maryland, Delaware Virginia, and they were so generous with their time and their gifts. I guess when I had visitors in the hospital; they saw I was having beer three times a day, so each visit brought a case of beer. I had enough beer in the dining room stacked by the wall to open my own brewery. (Unfortunately by this time beer tasted like medicine and I really didn't want to have anything to do with it. It would be about five years before I would enjoy a cold beer.)

Get well cards and well wishes filled the wall of the living room. The phone rang off its hook with people asking if there was anything we needed or anything they could do to help.

The newspaper came and did an article on my survival, which embarrassed me greatly. They took pictures, which I really didn't want, but felt I owed to the people for all their generosity, so they could see how happy I was.

Line crews would stop by during the day when they were working in the area and spend a few minutes with us. They always left with the statement, "If you need anything, give us a call."

Christmas was just a few days away. With the help of Jeanie and Peggy, Micki took quick shopping trips in preparation for the old man with a white beard. The house was all decorated and full of Christmas spirit. Dan and Rob were telling anyone who would listen just how good they had been.

Micki and I were both excited about having the Christmas holidays together with our children. We had been scared this would never happen again. The Christmas tree, which had been donated to us by Bunkie Austin, a man I worked with at Delmarva power, was beautiful. So you can just imagine how special this Christmas was—the laughter at our little boys' enthusiasm tearing open the gifts and squealing with happiness. I think they were just as excited about being home again and as we were.

Micki sat on the floor by the tree handing out one present at a time. Money was tight, so there weren't that many and she was making it last as long as possible.

There were four very happy people in a little white bungalow on Hayward Ave. in Fruitland, Maryland. Christmas was now over... most toys were sort of put away... as only a two-year-old and a five-year-old can do.

New Year's Eve came quickly and we celebrated with a great Eastern shore dinner. Micki is a great cook... and to think she could put a crust on a cup of coffee when we first got married.

We lay there listening to the fireworks going off at midnight just holding each other, knowing the boys were snug in their beds with Taffy guarding them.

* * *

Time passed too quickly. Soon it was time for me to return to the hospital.

By the middle of January, Micki received a call from Dr. Jabaley telling her an ambulance would pick me up in two days and take me to Children's Hospital on Green Spring Ave. in Baltimore.

Micki's mom and dad picked the boys up but just for a weekend this time. Micki couldn't stay with me because Dan was now in kindergarten and it was important for the boys to have as normal a life as possible. So it was their turn to be taken care of instead of me, and I would make out fine.

Micki rode in the ambulance with me and took the bus home. We made the trip in record time, even though the driver had to stop and give me oxygen because I became car sick after having lay in the bed for so long.

We arrived at Children's Hospital safe and sound. As I was wheeled into the hospital, we were met by two nurses—one black and one white. Mrs. Harrison and Mrs. Clunk were their names.

Mrs. Harrison, the black one, asked, "Where are you from?"

Fruitland Maryland, on the Eastern shore," I told her.

With that she gave me a big hug and kissed my cheek. Then she leaned over and whispered, "Don't worry, honey. It won't rub off."

I laughed out loud and the friendship between the three of us began at that very moment.

Mrs. Harrison and Mrs. Clunk were at my bedside more than any other hospital personnel. They learned all about Micki and me, our boys, and yes, Hammie.

I told them about her over and over, even the way she used to talk to me, like when I didn't want to do what she told me. She would be patient for a while and then with a hand on her hip and a finger in the air she would say, "Mr. Buck, if you don't do what I tell you to, I am going to smack your white ass!" As only she could say with that soft southern drawl. Then I knew I was in trouble and did what she said.

She had a way with words in three stages— joking, serious, and damn serious. When damn serious got there, you had better move, or else. I never found out what *or else* was.... I moved. God love you, Hammie.

* * *

In Children's Hospital I was placed in a semiprivate room and back on the circle electric bed. Dr. Jabaley entered my room and welcomed us back to Baltimore.

The reason for the change in hospitals was that this was an orthopedic hospital and I was going to have quite a few operations dealing with bone. And ~~plus~~ since I was no longer critical, I did not need Johns Hopkins.

I was now in serious but stable condition and during the next few weeks, I would be having a series of skin graft and reconstruction operations. This was the reason for the circle electric bed—to lessen the chances of bed sores by turning frequently.

Micki stayed at the bed and breakfast across the street when she came on the weekend to visit me. It seemed so strange and lonely not to have her with me every day. This was the first time we had been apart.

The operations seemed to be going very well. I looked so forward to the weekend when Micki would come up and tell me all the news about Danny and Robbie.

I had news for her. One of the nurses came in my room and told me there was a very famous person across the hall from me. It was Gino Marchetti, the famous linebacker of the Baltimore Colts who was now in the Hall of Fame. Holy Cow! Gino Marchetti! I almost fell out of bed I was so excited. I couldn't wait to tell Micki. He was coming in that day and so was she.

You have to know something about Micki.... she has never met a stranger in her life. Let it be the president of the United States, a Queen, or a derelict—it doesn't matter; she treats them all the same. She can be in an elevator and go three floors and have made a lifelong friend. So, as soon as I told her, out the door she went.

A few minutes later, she returned with the biggest damn man I had ever seen. He walked over to my bed, held out his hand and said, "Hi, Ed, my name is Gino. How are you? Your wife tells me you have had one hell of an experience."

"Yes-s-s-s sir," I said, shaking a hand that felt like a tennis racket.

He said it looked like we were going to be hospital buddies for a while. But he was in for an operation on his foot, which had been broken in the last game he played. I was still in shock at seeing this man I had seen on television so many times. The Colts were *my* team!

The next day Gino came into my room while Dr. Jabaley was there and said, "Hi, Doc. Is it okay for my buddy to have a little bit of drink?"

Dr. Jabaley asked him what he had in mind.

Gino replied, "Just a little bit of whiskey."

Dr. Jabeley looked at Gino and then into my thirsty eyes and said, "A little bit will be okay, but not much."

Things were looking up at this hospital stay!

The next day Gino came into my room and asked, "Do you like Italian subs? Not those so-called Italian subs but the real deal. We were to have subs and a little something to drink."

My roommate, Jim, whose last name escapes me, was as happy as I was.

The next thing we knew, two cases of beer, one case of whiskey and a cardboard box were delivered to our room. The cardboard box was full of the largest Italian subs I had ever seen! They were about 18 inches long—hard rolls filled with all the best kinds of meats—real Italian meats and cheeses, lettuce, tomato pickles, and even hot peppers.

Gino said, "It's Friday night and they aren't going to do anything to us on the weekend. So, let's party!"

This made Jim and me ecstatic!

Gino passed out the subs to each of us. Then he handed us an ice cold beer. Strange how beer, which had tasted like medicine, now tasted really good with that sub.

Gino sat down and we started talking. He wanted to know all about me and the accident. I wanted to talk about football and hear all about his career. But he insisted I talk first, so I told him it was like this... that on July 27 I had a rather shocking experience.

He laughed and said, "Micki told me that you took 69,000 volts of electricity three times.

"Yes, that's true," I said. "I was just not fast enough to get out of the way on the second and third time. You see the relays on the circuit breaker or re-closing device operate at zero seconds, three seconds and 15 seconds. You might say that I needed more time to make up my mind to get the hell out of the way."

Gino and Jim were both interested in hearing the details of what happened. Then we finally talked about football and different players on the Baltimore Colts team that I had grown up watching.

The dinner trays were delivered to each of us but we decided to keep drinking the beer and whiskey, eating the giant subs, and telling all kinds of stories. This continued until around 10 PM, when the supervisor of nurses told Gino he would have to go back to his own room.

Jim was sound asleep. I, on the other hand, wanted to continue. You see, by now I was paralyzed from head to toe. I couldn't feel a thing, but I sure felt good. All I wanted to do was talk and sing, and to be honest I can't carry a note in a water bucket.

Gino was riding up and down the hall in his wheelchair yelling "Yipee!" The nurse told him to go back to his room, but he would have nothing of that. When she became insistent, he continued down the hall saying, "Nurse, you'd better be careful or I will buy this place turn it into a Gino's and fire you all!"

I don't think she was amused.

The next day, Sunday, all of us were not very pretty to look at. Jim's and my room was a trash dump. The trashcans were filled with beer and whiskey bottles, and sub wrappers and papers were all over the floor.

Then trouble came. A nurse came in with the morning meds, took one look around and went through the ceiling. Next came the supervisor of nurses. She, too, went through the ceiling. I, on the other hand, still drunk, could only laugh.

She wanted to know who was responsible for this mess. I told her I did it. Somehow she did not believe me when she said that I was confined to a circle electric bed and paralyzed.

Gino, next-door in his room, could hear all the commotion. He staggered across the hallway, leaned on one side of the door and said, "What the hell is going on in here?"

The nursing supervisor turned around to see the monster leaning half in and half out of the door. He soon took responsibility for the whole mess and by looking at his size; she decided it was in her best interest to let it go.

Personnel were dispatched to clean the room and all was back to normal. Later the nurses who were told of our party and the good time we had even saw all the humor in the event.

* * *

During the afternoon Gino had several visitors whom he brought over to visit Jim and me. It was then that I got to meet people like Don Shula, and Ordell Bracey, Hall of Fame players and coaches from the Baltimore Colts football team.

I was in seventh heaven just to be able to shake hands with these talented, talented people. I got to meet the real deal. I played high school football and I was a fair player, but next to these guys I was just a wanna be. These guys had been there and done things I could only dream of.

On Sunday evening, the doctors made their nightly rounds in preparation for Monday surgeries. With the door of our room open, I could hear some conversation in Gino's room across the hall. I heard a rather loud and stern voice say, "What the hell are you talking about?"

A little while later Gino came into our room and asked, "Do you know what they just told me?"

I lay there are my circle electric bed smiling and said, "No, Gino. What did they tell you?"

He puffed up like a big teddy bear. "They said I have to wear a diaper when I go to the operating room. I told them it is not going to happen. There isn't a person big enough in this hospital to put a diaper on me."

After he left the room, Jim and I laughed until we cried. We had both been there. This was hospital policy; everyone going into surgery had to wear a diaper.

The next morning with our door open, upon request, Jim and I lie there in bed listening. Sure enough we could hear, "What the hell are you doing?" Then all got quiet.

The next day when Micki came up for a visit, as she was walking down the Hall past Gino's room, he called to her. (I had already told her what happened the night before when we spoke on the phone.

She thought it was so funny.) He told her in very quiet voice, "Do
you know what they did to me? They put a diaper on me and they
had to use of a bath blanket because a regular one wouldn't fit."

He was so indignant. Micki couldn't wait to get over to our room
and tell us. It was so funny.

All too soon, Gino's foot had healed and he left.. He had made
this hospital stay so bearable.

The day he was discharged he came into our room to say goodbye.
This was a happy/sad occasion. We were glad he got to go home
but at the same time would miss the excitement he brought into our
lives. Micki and I knew we had had the honor of meeting one of the
greatest football players in history and enjoyed his company to the
fullest. We will always remember those good times.

Jim left the same day as Gino, so now I was left on my own.

The next afternoon a huge basket was delivered to my room. It
was full of all kinds of fruit and beautifully wrapped candy. There
was a card in it from Gino, saying how much he had enjoyed meeting
me and spending time with my lovely wife and me.

If Gino should ever read this book; I feel I will be a dead man for
telling this story about him. It was just too much fun, buddy; I just
had to put it in print. I hope you understand and approve. Thanks for
the great memories.

The days were now long and it was back to the different surgeries.
Dr. Jabeley and Dr. Hanson were reconstructing the area for my right
ear, which had been burned off.

In the operating room, I remember Dr. Hanson standing by my
side saying, "Friends, Romans and Countrymen build me an ear!"

This surgery, even though I was awake during all of it, started
off with a good laugh. The sight of the large needles being placed in
different locations in my head was difficult to watch. Too bad there
were so many mirrors and I was so nosy.

Soon all of the right side of my head was numb and surgery began. I heard and felt all of the cutting and sewing. There was no pain, for which I was thankful.

Within a few days I was back in the operating room for surgery on my right hip. This area had been badly burned and required what is known as a flap surgery. This means relocating a portion of flesh and muscle in order to close an opened burned area. Then a long, boring hospital stay was required for the healing process to take place.

After several weeks, the doctors determined that the right ear construction was not healing properly. To prevent infection from setting in, it was necessary that the new ear be removed. So they repeated the same procedure with all the needles to the head. We were all disappointed.

I had been in the hospital for nearly 3 months and Dr. Jabaley felt it was time for me to go home and recharge my batteries. This made Micki and me very happy. I missed my family and home so much. So we said goodbye to Mrs. Harrison and Mrs. Clunk, and took another fast ride home in the ambulance.

It's surprising how everything got back to normal within a few days—at least as normal as it can be under the circumstances. Micki, now the head doctor and nurse, took care of all the bandages and dressings 24 hours a day, seven days a week. Between taking care of the two boys, cleaning the house and cooking for all of us, she still had to monitor my condition. This meant she had to change my body position every four hours around-the-clock.

In order to prevent additional bedsores, she would also change the sheets every four hours. This meant additional laundry.

She would lie down on the sofa in the living room and take a nap while keeping an eye and ear out for any the needs I might have. She never went to her own bed. For the life of me, I don't know how she did it. Yet she always had a great sense of humor and the biggest smile you ever saw, with a constant positive attitude.

I was enough to handle by myself, let alone taking care of two very active little boys. How could one human being be so strong? If there is such a thing as a guardian angel, I was lucky enough to have married mine. There has to be something to predestination; I am not smart enough to have chosen a lifelong companion that great.

It was becoming perfectly clear to me that I was not going to die; she was not going to let me take the easy way out of the situation. We were going to go the distance together, no matter how long it took.

After a month at home, we returned to Children's Hospital. It seemed like just yesterday the ambulance brought me home, and now it was taking me back.

The ride was quick as always, and Mrs. Harrison and Mrs. Clunk greeted our return with a lot of hugs.

This time I was in a room with a retired fireman by the name of Dan Holden. Dan had been a captain with the Baltimore City Fire Department. And for the next few weeks Dan and his family would become good friends with Micki and me.

This return trip to Children's Hospital was for one main reason and that was the reconstruction of my left elbow. The bone chips, as the result of the electrical shock, had solidified within the elbow. It was a solid mass and required surgery.

Dr. Jabaley had advised me of an orthopedic surgeon by the name of Dr. Gibson Packard, who would perform the surgery.

"Is he any good?" I asked.

"Well, he worked on Elizabeth Taylor. I think he's good enough for you," he replied.

We had a good laugh about that.

Doctor Packard arrived the next day, dressed in a suit and looking like something out of Hollywood. Clean-cut. Sharp as a razor, he was soft-spoken but stern. Yet, he was very much like Dr. Jabaley said he was—very easy to communicate with.

He checked my arms and the x-rays and then proceeded to tell me what he was going to do. He told me I had two choices. They could either provide me with the elbow movement of 120° extension and be able to touch my chin or 90° and extended all the way out to a straight arm. I said I preferred 120° angle, because that way shaving would not be a problem.

The following day, the surgery was completed without a hitch. Doctor Packard was very happy with the end result of his work.

Now came the healing time. I had to follow his instructions to the letter.

Doctor Packard was very well known and liked throughout the hospital. He was affectionately known as Dr. Gibby Packard. Talk about being talented. He was not only an outstanding surgeon; he loved to ride motorcycles, played concert piano and an electric guitar.

One day the orderly assigned to our area, Nathaniel, or Nat for short, came into our room. He asked Dan and me if we would like to hear some music. We both said yes. It would be so great to relieve the boredom.

Nat left and returned with his electric guitar. This was in the afternoon, Dan and I had just been lying there resting and talking, sipping on a glass of Southern comfort, which someone had left lying around unattended. Nat plugged in his guitar, placed his foot on the chair, the guitar on his right leg and tuned it to his satisfaction.

Dan and I held our glasses high and said, "Let the music began!"

Nat played some great music.

The afternoon was quiet. We were enjoying the company and the refreshments when who should walk in but Dr. Packard. You could've heard a pin drop.

Nat had the fear of God on his face, while Dan and I were trying to hide our good old Southern comfort glasses.

Dr. Packard looked at Nat and said, "So you play the guitar?"

"Yes Sir," Nat said. "Hope you don't mind my playing a little music for the guys."

Dr. Packard smiled and said, "Not at all. May I see your guitar?"

Nat handed the guitar to Dr. Packard, who ran his hand across the strings, looked at Nat and said, "You're left-handed aren't you?"

"Yes," Nat replied.

Dr. Packard changed from his right to his left hand and began playing the guitar. The man was phenomenal. He could play with either hand.

Nat, Dan and I watched and listened. I wondered what the hell else he could do. But then I didn't want to know. At this time I was feeling pretty stupid.

When the music ended Dr. Packard checked my left arm. He was satisfied with the progress but was keeping an eye on some hematoma in the area. I remember him telling me that in college, he had trouble remembering the word *hematoma* so he would call it hemo-tomato.

His strict instructions were I was not to move the arm for any reason for several days. It had to heal and in just a certain position.

He checked me every day. On the third day, I removed the sling that held my hand and forearm, pulled it up close to my chest, and ever so gently moved my elbow. There was absolutely no pain and it moved so smoothly. I was so happy to be able to move my elbow again. Then I replaced the sling carefully so you could not tell I had moved it.

Dr. Packard came in the next morning, removed the bandages partially, looked me in the eye and said, "So, you had to move your arm. Why? I thought I told you not to move that arm for any reason."

Totally embarrassed, I knew that lying was not an option. "Yes, I had moved it, but I promise I won't move it again until you tell me to." I said.

He told me no damage had taken place but if I continued to move it, all the progress I had made would be lost. Believe me; the next time the elbow moved, Dr. Packard moved it. Finally when the slings and bandages were removed the arm was working perfectly, just as he had promised.

During the healing process Dan Holden and his wife Wilso, and their daughters Anita, Rosella, Caroline and son Ricky became good friends.

During the months we were in the hospital, in order to alleviate the boredom, we liked to play tricks on the nurses every chance we got. One prank I remember distinctly was taking a sterile glass container that was used for a urine sample, filling it about halfway with water and Southern Comfort to resemble the color of the real thing, and setting it on the tray. When the nurse came in, she picked it up and asked me what it was for.

I took it from her hand and said, "By the looks of it, I'd better run it through again," as I raised it to my mouth and drank it.

The look of horror on her face, was followed by gales of laughter from Dan and me. Then when Dan and I told her what we had done, she laughed, but I'm not sure she was as amused as we were.

Our reputations spread throughout the floor rather quickly. So we only did this stunt once. But it was all taken in good fun; they knew we were trying to bring some laughter into our rather drab lives at that time.

The days and weeks weren't moving as quickly as I would have liked, because I had been in the hospital for three months. I had several different surgeries after the main surgery on my left elbow—more flap surgeries, and skin grafting.

Finally Dr. Jabaley Okayed my going home to recharge the batteries. And again it was a rather bittersweet time, because saying goodbye to Dan and his family was hard. I thanked them for the great friendship that had made my time in the hospital go by so much easier. We made plans to visit each other and to keep in touch, and we did for many years.

Summer was on the way. It was our hope that I could remain home for the summer while our boys were out of school.

The insurance company provided me with a patient lift. Micki used this to pick me up out of the bed and placed me in the wheelchair. My arms were still too weak and I had to be pushed wherever I went. This required a lot of effort and time for Micki to take care of me. Still, she never complained and maintained a continuous positive attitude. I, on the other hand, was getting sick and tired of being dependent. I was used to helping other people, not being the one in need of help.

Every day Micki got me dressed and up into the chair for an hour or two. One morning I woke up with a fever, and when Micki took my temperature, it was 103 and rising.

She called Johns Hopkins hospital and talked to the doctor on call. She told him that my temperature was rising and there were red marks starting at my ankle and running up my leg. The temperature now was 105°.

He told her to place ice bags on the back of my neck, under each arm, under my scrotum and to call for an ambulance at once.

By now I was as hot as hell. My eyes could not focus properly and I had a terrible headache. The ice bags just made things more uncomfortable because at the same time I was hot and shivering from cold. I felt sick and nauseated but did not throw up.

The ambulance arrived in record time and I sat on my way to the hospital. My temperature now was 106°.

When I arrived, they promptly put me in a better vice. IVs were started while in the ambulance and antibiotics were administered as soon as I arrived at the hospital.

Dr. Breal assured me that the antibiotics were the big guns, so to speak. He told me I had phlebitis in my left leg and that the condition was very serious. Had Micki not taken action when she did, I would have died.

Within 24 hours, the fever had broken and I was transferred to a normal bed. I was happy to get out of the ice. The medication was doing the job it was designed for, and I was finally discharged within just a few days.

* * *

The phone rang one morning and I heard Micki say, "Yes, this is the Buck residence."

She handed me the phone and told me that someone wanted to speak to me.

The male voice said, "You don't know me. My name is Steady Smith. I would like to talk to you."

"About what?" I asked.

"Your condition," he answered. "I understand that you're paralyzed."

I told him yes, but it was only temporary. It would be gone within six months.

"How long have you been in this condition?" he inquired.

I had to stop to think, because it would be one year in August. Maybe God had not looked at his calendars, because six months had gone by and I was still paralyzed.

"May I come over to your house to visit you?" he asked.

I was not in the mood to meet strangers who would come to the house to stare at me and my condition. But when he told me he was also in a wheelchair and would like to meet me that perked my curiosity.

I agreed to his request, although I really didn't want this meeting. It was going to be a waste of time.

I was about to meet one of the most courageous human beings I will ever meet in my lifetime. And one who would change my life dramatically.

A few days later a rather short man in a wheelchair was sitting beside my bed. He told me his name was Steady Smith and that he heard a lot about me and wanted to meet me. He told me that his father was a doctor so he knew a lot about what was happening to me at Johns Hopkins Hospital. Plus, there had been quite a few write-ups in the local paper and he had been following my progress.

Knowing that we lived so close; he wanted to get to know me. He proceeded to tell me that he had been in a wheelchair since birth and he was also paralyzed.

Although I found his story interesting I could still not see that we had anything in common. After all, I didn't become paralyzed until I was 25 years old. He, on the other hand, had never walked, so how could he know of my problems?

After about an hour of conversation, he said it was time for him to leave and asked if he could return some time.

"Sure," I said. "It's always good to have company."

I really liked the guy.

After he left. I told Micki, "I wonder why he wants to become friends with me."

She said," I don't know. He seems like a very nice guy, but we don't know anything about him except his name."

But that was just beginning...

Lying in bed so much, I was becoming weaker and weaker. The only way I could sit up in bed was to have the head portion cranked up and pillows placed behind me.

I started to get into a deep state of depression. I was making one negative statement after another. Micki did her best to keep my attitude positive, but her attempts weren't working.

Steady called and asked if he could come over.

"Sure, what the hell, I can't feel any worse," I said in my now usual bitter tone.

When he arrived, it took very little time for him to see my mental attitude. When he asked me what was wrong, I told him my level of paralysis is T/6 and that he wouldn't understand.

"Mine is the same. So, what's the problem?"

"I can't do anything for myself. Micki has to do everything."

He looked at me and asked, "Do you want to do anything for yourself?"

"Hell yes!" I responded with anger. I thought, *Who the hell does he think he is, talking to me like that in my condition? Doesn't he realize I'm much worse off than he is?*

He positioned his chair, locked his wheels and placed his hand through my bed rail. He said, "Give me your hand."

I looked at him with doubt. "Why?"

He asked, "Do you want to sit up or are you scared?"

I could feel my temperature-rising. He was talking to me like I was afraid, like I was a little boy who needed mommy to do everything for him.

I put my hand in his and he told me to squeeze. Within a second I was sitting up great in bed.

Now I was scared. *How the hell did he do that?* I wondered.

He kept me in that position for a few minutes and then gently laid me back down again.

"Do you want to do more?" Steady asked.

"Like what?"

I suddenly wanted to hear what else he had to say. He had my undivided attention. He had earned it.

Steady stayed and talked for over an hour. He showed us how he did wheelies in the wheelchair, which took our breath away, and told us of other things that he did by himself.

He took care of himself and was totally independent. He drove his own car, he fished from his own boat, and he went deer hunting with bow and arrow.

After he left, I told Micki I had just met Superman.

My attitude was changing and I began to think about physical rehabilitation, but I knew I wasn't close to being ready yet. Steady had given me the ability to have goals in my mind—something to work for, a reason to think positively.

* * *

During this time, several different people entered my life, and had a great impact on me. Steady was the first who would change my life dramatically. The next one was the managers of the Suburban Gas Company, Harold Powell; he heard that I was interested in radios. This, too, was a great interest for him.

He visited me and while talking he said that he would be coming back with something for me. He returned a few days later with a crystal radio he had built.

It was about the size of a box of kitchen matches. It had no batteries or any power source, and I wondered how it worked. Herald proudly proceeded to tell me it was all about his construction project.

He placed a set of old military headphones on my head and proceeded to hook a long wire to our sink faucet in the kitchen and another wire scotch taped to the wall and above the windows around the living room.

We just looked at him quizzically.

Suddenly I could hear the local radio station WBOC loud and clear. *Wow, this is really neat* I thought.

Herald told me he had made it for me and that this was mine to keep. I couldn't believe he was being so generous.

I lay in bed and listened to the radio station hour after hour.

Bob Terry, a lineman with Delmarva power, heard about Herald's project and gift. Bob was an amateur radio operator with a call sign WA3CGT. He stopped by with an amateur radio receiver, a Hammerlund HQ-180. This was huge in size, and I knew nothing about it.

Bob spent several hours teaching me how to operate this fantastic radio receiver. After a few days of listening to the ham radio operators, my interest in amateur radio became very strong.

I talked to Herald about it. He suggested I get some books on the subject and start reading. I had plenty of time on my hands; I sure wasn't going anywhere. So I not only got books on ham radio, I enrolled in a correspondence course with the National Radio Institute in Washington, DC. The course was on complete radio communications. I thought this would be a good start since it covered all areas of radio communications.

I then purchased two 78 rpm records from the Heathkit Company. These I hoped would help me learn the Morse code.

For the next several months, I studied the books and learned as much as I could. I even took them to the hospital and studied there.

* * *

That summer had a bright spot, thanks to our great neighbor, Bob Tarr.

Danny was playing peewee league baseball, and I so badly wished I could go to one of his games. I loved sports; I had played baseball and football all during my growing up years. So to be unable to watch my little boy play broke my heart. Micki would come home and tell me about the game and although I enjoyed it, it wasn't the same.

Then one day I heard a commotion in the front yard...Micki had gotten me up earlier and dressed so I was sitting in my wheelchair just watching television.

Bob Tarr came to the house with his old beat up Dodge pickup truck. He backed it up to our front porch, got out and put the tailgate down. Then he placed two boards from the porch to the bed of his truck. He then came into the house.

"Ed, you're going to the ballpark," he announced.

"No way," I said.

"Danny is playing peewee baseball and you're going to go see him. Don't you want to?"

I was excited yet scared.

He loaded me in the back of a pickup and off we went at a blistering speed of about 10 or 15 miles an hour. I held on for dear life to anything I could get my hands on. I thought I was going to die we were going so fast.

Bob had one eye on the road and the other on me. He just laughed at the fear written all over my face.

We arrived at the ballpark about half a mile away from our house. Three ball fields were full of children. Dan was in one of them.

Bob positioned the truck so that I could see the game perfectly. I watched my son's concentrated interest in the outfield—oh, not in baseball; he was mainly interested in watching cars or planes go by.

When a ball would be hit to him, I would yell, "Danny, Danny! Wake up! It went past you."

I asked other loving parents where the parents of that boy in the outfield were. - I didn't want them to know that I was his daddy.

The parents would answer, "I don't know any of them. They must have been dropped here by mistake."

We all laughed at our some day superstars. This was a great experience for me to get out of the house and watch Danny start the process of growing up one day at a time. He mixed well with other children and developed long-lasting friendships.

Robbie was very busy in a mud puddle gathering up tadpoles. He had a love for animals, which he has carried through to this day.

The game was over an hour, and then we began the grueling ride back home. Bob drove like he had a crate of eggs in the back. He unloaded me safely on our front porch and a great day was complete.

Bob Tarr was a World War Two veteran and a heavy equipment operator with Delmarva Power. He was also very actively involved with the Fruitland Boy Scouts. He and Gene Shirk built the ramp for my wheelchair so I could access the sidewalk from the porch.

David Robinson, a fellow employee at Delmarva Power, heard that I really wanted to attend the company picnic; that was being held at the Hepburn carnival grounds and Hebron, Maryland. He brought his Volkswagen bus over to our house and left it there for us to use.

The day of the company picnic, I was loaded via a makeshift ramp into the VW bus. When we arrived at the picnic, there were enough men to manually lift me to the ground.

There I sat, right in the middle of all my friends from work. All the food was free and this was the home of the best oyster sandwiches on the Eastern shore of Maryland (along with the famous crab cake sandwiches, which were also excellent, and all kinds of hot dogs and hamburgers and every thing that a carnival would have).

While I enjoyed about three bottles of beer and two of the best oyster sandwiches in the world, I told more lies than you can shake a stick at. (When a group of lineman gets together; we talk about the truth and nothing but the truth. Now if you believe that, I have a bridge to sell you.) We talked about the times we had completed different jobs under the worst possible conditions, sunny days, and how good we were at our craft. We laughed until we cried when we knew one of us had told the best lie so far. Then the next truth teller took a turn. This continued all afternoon.

The children rode all the rides in a park, the wives played bingo and other games, while participating on the rides with the children. They also kept their eyes on us, because there was a beer truck with all the beer iced down.

When this day was complete I returned home paralyzed from head to toe, but the refreshments and seeing all the friends from work made this a day I'll always remember. It was also what I needed to boost my desire to get back into the mainstream of life.

My friends accepted the fact that I was now in a wheelchair. The paralysis might leave; if it didn't, I knew I still had friends.

There had to be something I could do at Delmarva Power from a wheelchair. Just the thought, for now, made having more surgery followed by physical therapy was now something that I would not dread.

Two neighbors who lived down the street, Burt Widdowson and Vernon Budd, heard I was becoming interested in radio. Burt was a dispatcher for the Maryland State Police and Vernon Budd, a local builder. Together they joined and purchased a Plectron police monitor for me so I could listen to the local police activities.

Now my interest in radio was getting higher and higher. I could now listen to the local radio station, thanks to Harold Powell, and ham radio, thanks to Bob Terry and the state police.

With all the radio activity and my studying the NRI radio communications course, I was running out of time to feel sorry for myself. Micki had placed a card table next to my bed—books, tools, and radios were placed on it. I could read, listen or try to repair a radio.

One day, during one of Gene Shirk's many visits; he laid a Chess set on the table. I knew nothing about the game of chess. Then he very patiently, over several weeks, taught me how to play the game but not well enough to beat him.

We talked about the accident and he told me things that had happened I didn't know about, since I was unconscious at the time. He told me details that would leave both of us crying our hearts out. It had not only been hard on me, but also on my friends with whom I worked so closely.

After several visits, I found out that Gene was now on medication for depression. Our visits had to stop for a time. Gene could no longer stand the psychological stress of seeing a perfectly healthy friend with whom he had worked so closely every day, now lying in a bed, helpless except for what others could do for him.

The doctor said the medicine would help, but separation from me was necessary.

When Gene told me this news, I understood. He had seen everything as it was happening and then was directly involved in the rescue. The sight and smell of the human flesh being burned alive is not easily forgotten. We both had to move on. We had to somehow put this behind us.

Parting was sad, but we both knew it was for the best.

With the company picnic now a memory, I was hungry for those oysters again.

Bob and Peggy Tarr came to the house with a bushel of oysters. Bob prepared them raw, steamed, and stewed as I lay in that bed proceeding to try to commit suicide by eating so many. I ate so many I dreamed of oysters that night. Everyone laughed at my ability to stuff so many in.

That summer had been great. I was able to get out of bed, go to the Little League games, and the company picnic.

Steady came around to offer little words of encouragement. "Come on, gimp. Let's go for a stroll down the street," he would say.

He had this thing about making me angry so that I would try harder to do what I just told him I couldn't. He kept on me until I did. Then he just sat there and smiled.

He would tell me, "All good things take time." He was always patient but insistent about different things he suggested I do. He must have seen something that I couldn't, for each day when he came over, I went a little further. And each night I slept like a baby.

At least now with Micki helping me to get into the chair, I could move myself around, though limited. Steady was still coming over frequently and calling me a gimp, telling me we were going for a walk.

What did he mean walk? I hadn't walked in a year.

But he laughed and said, "Okay, not to stretch your legs. We'll stretch your arms."

Down the road we went, Steady acting crazy like spinning his tires and doing wheelies, while I so carefully maneuvered my chair, watching out for any ruts or stones.

After watching him for a few minutes, I thought I could do the same. So I took off with everything I had my body. After about 50 feet, I thought I surely would have a heart attack.

Steady stopped to make sure I was all right. Assured that I was, he said, "Too

This went on for what I wish sure was hours, but Micki said was about 15 minutes.

Steady taunted me, calling me a gimp and asking me if I was just going to sit there.

Hell flew into me. I was not going to sit there like a good cripple.

"I'll catch you and pass you! You'll see," I said.

I pushed my body repeatedly with everything I had.

We returned home just before I was pronounced dead. I told Steady that someday I would make him pay for all that sadistic treatment he put me through.

He laughed. "You'll be okay once you get in shape. You just still have a ways to go. The question is, are you man enough to do it?"

He just never quit with his little digs.

* * *

One day Robbie, our youngest son, came to my bed with tears in his eyes. He said someone had just come to our house and drove off in our car. He wanted it back; he didn't know what was happening to his car.

I called for Micki and asked her if she knew anything about this. She said it was being taken to the garage for repairs.

A few days later Micki got me to rest and in a wheelchair early in the day, I asked her why I had to get up so early. She said she just wanted to change my schedule a little.

Soon after I was up and in my wheelchair, there was a knock on the front door. When she opened it, Francis McKee (or Mac as he was affectionately known) entered. He was the head of the stations department of Delmarva Power and Light. And with him was H. Ray Landon, the head of the personnel department.

I was used to seeing Mac just about every week. He brought my paycheck, unless he was out of town. Then someone else would bring it. I never missed a paycheck in all the months I was out.

But I wondered what Ray and Mac were doing here. I would soon find out the answer to that question.

Mac McKee, and Ray Landon said they had something outside that they wanted us to see. The door was opened and as I went out and down the ramp, I could see a brand-new 1968 Volkswagen bus.

This bus had a sliding side door and a fold-down aluminum ramp. There were other men standing beside it—Georgia Siever, radio technician, and Ernie Nichols, line Foreman.

They all welcomed Micki, Danny, Robbie and me to our new VW bus. They told us about the Southern Division employee's fundraiser and what it had accomplished. They told us of all the contributions throughout the state of Delaware, Maryland and Virginia. From the highest executive to the custodian, they all wanted to participate in helping with my recovery.

They spent considerable time showing Micki how everything worked. They even got her to demonstrate her proficiency in getting me in and out of the bus. After all, she was the captain of this new ship. Again, everything fell on her shoulders.

George Sievers gave me a demonstration of the new Lafayette 525 radio. Now I could not only listen to the radio; I could talk on it as well.

After all instructions of safety and operation of the equipment were completed, Micki and I just held each other and said, "Thank you so much for everything." We were so grateful and the thank you was from the bottom of our hearts.

I remember when Ray, Mac, George and Ernie laughed and went back to work, I just sat there thinking, *This is the sign that I will never walk again. And I worry how much more can Micki stand. She is my wife, nurse, housekeeper, and now chauffeur for me, a cripple.*

Now reality set in. Micki would have to drive the bus. It was standard shift transmission and I, being paralyzed, could never drive it.

All of those things I would worry about later. It was time to get in and take a ride.

Micki attached my wheelchair to a fabricated cable assembly and pushed a button. The internal mounted electric winch pulled me up the ramp and into the bus. The boys were so excited about taking a ride with both Mommy and Daddy.

We were all on her maiden voyage. We traveled about 45 miles to Ocean View, Delaware. This was where Micki's mom and dad lived.

Boy, were they happy to see us. I couldn't wait to tell them about Micki's driving. They got a big laugh out of my greatly exaggerated details, like the one about driving like Mario Andretti behind the steering wheel of an 18 wheeler, while sipping on a beer, and that I had been so scared.

I know they saw right through me, since Micki was a teetotaler. And Danny and Robbie were quick to tell on me.

We talked and laughed and had a wonderful dinner. And then it was time to return home. I told them I would give them a call when we got home and let them know if I lived through another stress test of Micki's driving. (All joking aside, she's the most safety-conscious driver I have ever been around. To think I said that and not being under the influence of something is scary.)

Actually we arrived home safely and sat and talked about how overwhelmed we were with the VW bus and how all the employees' contributions made this possible.

When we went to bed that night, neither of us could sleep.

As the days went on, we started traveling to different parts on the Delmarva Peninsula, showing off our new bus. We tried to go to every Delmarva Power and Light office to show the bus and tell people how grateful we were.

Steady came over, and I told him all about the bus and how nice it was for us to be able travel. We soon went to his house—all four of us, and we met his father, Dr. Stedman Smith, and his wife, Dorothy, who was also a nurse. They made us feel welcome.

We visited with them many times and enjoyed their company immensely.

* * *

Another extraordinary person was Dr. Robert Atkins, a doctor who cared as much about his patients as he did about himself. He made house calls—a lost art nowadays, and came to our house many times.

Danny and Robbie called him *Dr. Donald Duck* because he talked in a duck voice to them. They loved him so much and were never afraid to go to his office.

On one of his many visits, he saw an area that might become a potential problem on my right hip. He kept an eye on it and told me to keep it clean until I could return to the hospital.

I went back to Children's Hospital in preparation for surgery on my ear. This time I did not have to go in an ambulance; Micki drove us in our brand-new Volkswagen Bus. It seemed so strange to be able to sit up and ride all the way to Baltimore. (I hope no one else has to find out how important it is to sit up.)

I knew my way through Johns Hopkins and Children's Hospital by looking at the ceiling and the lights. When you are always on your back, this is all you can see. So I actually enjoyed the trip back to Baltimore.

When we arrived, the doctors and nurses were very happy with our new bus and how Micki could handle everything.

* * *

While preparing for the surgery, I got staph infection in my right hip, and my fever shot to 105°. The nurses placed me in a private room where everything was sterile. The doctors and nurses or anyone else who came in my room had to wear sterile gowns and masks.

The nurses were so concerned with my fever; they didn't leave my room and stayed in constant contact with the doctors. When the temperature climbed to 106°, the nurse obtained permission to give me five aspirin. And, of course, I was on another bed of ice.

Finally, the fever broke and antibiotics controlled the infection. A few days later, surgery on the hip was completed and all was well in that area. Reconstruction of the ear was put on hold.

Over the next several weeks, this skin grafting continued, and plans were again made for the reconstruction of my right ear. This time I would be able to enjoy Thanksgiving and Christmas at home.

Micki came to get me in our new bus and the trip home was enjoyable except for crossing the Chesapeake Bay Bridge. Back then there was only one bridge. The new one was under construction. As we were crossing it, we had to stop on the very top of the bridge for a caravan of tractor-trailers loaded with explosives, which had the right-of-way, to cross.

As we sat there and watched each tractor-trailer pass, the bridge would literally shake with each passing. It was then I realized I had a very serious fear of heights. I could look out the window, and I found myself wanting to get out of the wheelchair and get down on the floor.

My forehead, hands and arms began to shake and sweat. Micki talked to me, trying to calm me down. But I could not talk I was scared. I realized my legs would not move. This meant I could no longer support myself in the steel structures as I had before the accident.

I felt worthless. *What would I or could I do if something went wrong up there?* That helpless feeling lasted for a long time.

The trucks passed and we continued toward home, but it took a while for things to get back to normal.

* * *

Christmas was right around the corner and Micki did some shopping. Only this time, I was tagging along. I think I was more trouble than help. I wanted to buy one of everything. However, we could afford very little.

Christmas was a wonderful time with family and friends—the smell of Christmas dinner cooking, the gaily wrapped presents under the tree, the house decorated with streamers that Robbie and Danny made by taking pieces of construction paper and gluing them together into a paper chain. (They were so proud of the red and green paper chains that adorned the ceiling in the living room.) The money might not have been there, but the Christmas spirit was abundant.

Before we knew it, January of 1969 was upon us and it was again time to load up and return to the hospital. That trip completed my surgeries.

I had the option of more surgery on my right ear, as the cartilage had been removed from my right chest area. This cartilage was later shaped to reform an ear. It was then placed under the skin in the area of my right ear. However, blood in the area where the cartilage had been removed became infected.

Dr. Jabaley opened the area and removed the hematoma. He packed the incision with medicated gauze. He then showed Micki what she would have to do over the next several weeks.

Anyone looking down into the incision could actually see my heart beat.

A young intern assisting Dr. Jabaley asked Micki if she was a nurse.

"No, I'm not," she said.

The young doctor said, "The depth of the incision is only 2 cm from the heart. I would not send him home with anyone short of being a registered nurse."

"Micki has had more nurse's training in the past year with this patient than most nurses receive in four years," Dr. Jabaley replied. "I have the utmost confidence in her in that she will do fine."

The young doctor just looked at Micki and said, "You sure are some kind of woman."

Micki just smiled. "Not to worry. If I don't like what I see, I will call Dr. Jabaley right away."

We packed up and headed for home again. After about a week Micki told me that she did not like the way things were healing...that she smelled infection. I trusted her judgment.

When she called Dr. Jabeley and told him that she was bringing me back because there was a problem; he immediately said he would meet us in the emergency room.

The boys went to Peggy's house to spend the night.

We got into the bus and made a hurried trip in Baltimore. When we arrived in the emergency room, Dr. Jabaley was waiting for us. That same young intern was with him as they put me on the table.

When they opened my shirt, Dr. Jabaley took a pair of Kelly's sterile gauze pads and punctured the area. Hematoma (blood and infection) actually hit the ceiling, there was so much pressure.

The young intern looked at Micki and said, "Now I see why Dr. Jabaley let him go home with you."

After they again packed the area with the medicated gauze, we were allowed to go home. This time it healed perfectly.

I later contacted Dr. Jabaley and told him that I had had enough surgery. We would forget the surgery on the ear. If it was not life-threatening, I did not want it.

He totally understood. He said the surgery would make only a minor improvement. He said, "If you change your mind, give me a call. I will see you for a checkup and six months."

* * *

The next part of my rehabilitation was physical therapy. It was now the summer of 1969, and Ed Jones, my case manager, for the workers compensation insurance company, Aetna Life and Casualty, told me it was time for physical therapy. I told him I was progressing just fine and didn't need it. He said, after a heavy and undesirable discussion, I had two choices—either go to Montebello Hospital in Baltimore or Deer's Head Hospital in Salisbury, Maryland.

After several days discussion with Micki, I chose Deer's Head Hospital. I wanted to be close to home.

At this hospital I was introduced to Mrs. Florence Leist, head of the physical therapy department. After her examination of my physical condition, I asked her how long it would take me to go home. She said three or four months in the hospital.

I told her she didn't understand. I wasn't staying in the hospital but was going to do this as an outpatient. She refused to go along with my request.

I told her I would think about it, and I went home.

Ed Jennings had several meetings with me over the next week or so, and I finally agreed and returned to Deer's Head Hospital reluctantly.

I asked the physical therapist, what was the shortest time anyone had stayed in the hospital and accomplished what was necessary to be able to go home self sufficient? She said three months.

I told her, "I will beat that time frame. Now, let's get started."

Two therapist assistants by the names of Jake and Ed placed me on a mat on the floor. It was a padded, rectangular table about 20 inches high. They then placed a set of barbells with wheels to keep from crushing me on my chest.

The barbells added additional weight — about 26 pounds. I was told to do as many chest presses as I could. I completed five and thought I was going to have a heart attack.

Jake and Ed just laughed and said we had a long way to go but we would get there.

Monday through Friday they had me on the mats from early in the morning to late afternoon. The goal was to increase my strength to the maximum, generate and develop good balance techniques, be able to dress and undress myself, and to transfer in and out of a car.

Within the first week, I was able to press 50 pounds 50 times… just before I thought it would have heart failure (just kidding!). The second week I did 100 pounds 50 times.

The balance of tasks was coming along fine and dressing was less of a problem. I was now transferring from the bed to the wheelchair and vice versa, from the chair to the mat table, and finally to Mrs. Leist's car.

At the end of the third week, Jake and Ed called Mrs. Leist to the mat table. Jake told her to watch as I went through the balance techniques and transferred to the mat table from the chair. Then they loaded the barbells with 126 pounds of weight—because that was as much as they had—and I proceeded to do my chest presses 200 times without stopping.

Mrs. Leist grinned at me and said, "Mr. Buck, get out of here. I can do nothing further for you. You have completed everything in three weeks. I have never had anyone else do that. Congratulations. Come and see us from time to time."

The next week, guess who stopped by! Steady Smith, my nemesis. But I was ready and waiting.

When he arrived, he asked how I made out. I told him to follow me and said I would show him.

Down the ramp and out into the street we went. We went from one street to another as fast as it I could go, looking back and saying, "Come on, gimp! Keep up with me."

My arms and chest were now like the strongest iron.

Steady was not far behind. As he caught up he said, "Okay, where to now, Super Gimp? Show me what you can do."

With my newfound confidence, I took off with my front wheels in the air, going down the street and sliding sideways to a stop.

Steady smiled. I will never forget what he said; "Show off!" as he reached out his hand to shake mine. He congratulated me and said that he knew all along that I had what it took to succeed.

Steady and I returned home both tired and dirty.

We enjoyed many years together. Whenever I would get down in the dumps and needed to cry on his shoulder he was always there. I mean always, understanding and helpful.

This man had been given his last rites five times before he was 30 years of age. How could I not watch and listen to everything he did? He had been at death's door five times. A bigger, stronger, and gentler man I have never known.

Soon after Steady went home, I told Micki, "Remember when I told you I would make him pay for what he had put me through that day? Well, he is still the best, but I am right behind him and close on his wheels. He can't look back without looking me in the eye. He and I both feel good about that.

Many years later Steady got married to a wonderful lady named Esther. His wife was a quadriplegic; he took care of all her needs, from dressing and feeding her, to also taking care of himself.

Esther passed away suddenly in 2001 after many years of a loving marriage. I lost the best mentor a man could ever have in 2002. He was 55 years old and had been paralyzed since birth. We were in Florida at the time of his death; I didn't get to tell my brother in heart good-bye. The world had lost a great man, and I lost a great friend.

* * *

As the summer faded into the fall, it was time to plan to go back to work. I couldn't drive our VW bus due to the standards shift transmission.

We found a good use 1969 Ford galaxy 500 at a local used car lot. We purchased the two-door Ford at Mills Motors in Fruitland, Maryland.

The insurance company had hand controls placed on the vehicle so I could drive it. I had to contact the state of Maryland to get a learner's permit.

After obtaining a permit, Micki and I went for a ride. Only this time I was behind the wheel.

What a scary feeling, driving with only my hands. With hours of nervous tension and Micki's patience, I learned to handle the car safely with only my hands. It took months for me to stop trying to use my right foot, which was no longer there, to accelerate and break the vehicle.

We went to Glen Burnie, Maryland, and I was examined by a team of doctors and then was given my driving test, which I passed.

We returned home after completing one more step toward my returning to work.

In October, 1969, I got in my car and headed to the Delmarva Power main office building in Salisbury. With a body full of energy and now a fast wheelchair, I entered the building and went straight to the office of H. Ray Landon.

I rolled into his office and said, "Hello Ray. I am ready to come back to work."

He and Dorsey Marvel, secretary of I.B.E.W. local union 1307, stood and with smiles on their faces said "hi" to me and asked me how I was.

I told them both I had completed physical rehab and wanted to come back to work. After their congratulations of my accomplishments, they started discussing what jobs I could do in a wheelchair. They asked me what I wanted to do.

I said, "I didn't know. This is the first time in a wheelchair for me."

Ray said," Let him think about it and see what I can come up with. This is the first time anyone has ever returned to work in a wheelchair. We will have to work on this and get back to you."

Ray asked, "Have you taken a vacation?"

I looked at him and said, "I have been confined to bed for over two years. Isn't that vacation enough?"

Ray said, "No. I mean have you taken Micki and the boys out for a good time—maybe two weeks or so?"

I said, "No. I just want to get back to work as soon as possible."

Ray said, "That's great and I know you're ready. But after all, Micki and the boys have been through a rough time. So how about a vacation for them?

This did sound like a good idea. Ray said he would come to our house in December and talk to me about coming back to work on January 2, 1970.

I returned home to tell Micki we had a new problem called vacation.

Micki thought this was a great idea. Finally we would get a chance to relax and have a good time.

Where could we go with the boys that would be both fun and educational we wondered? We decided on the Luray Caverns along the Blue Ridge Parkway.

Micki, who can pack for a month within 15 minutes, was full of happiness. She of all people needed this vacation.

Within a few days we were off for the caverns and mountains of Virginia. We arrived late in the afternoon and found a nice motel on a hill overlooking the valley.

While Micki unpacked the car and made our room ready, I decided to take the boys for a stroll down a hill into the valley. Micki finished unpacking and caught up with us halfway down the hill.

I asked the boys if they wanted to race. Seemed like a good idea since we were all going downhill.

The boys took off like little rabbits and then I started as fast as I could go. I yelled to Micki to push because they were beating me. She did and then all hell broke loose.

My front wheels went into a gopher hole that was covered with grass. My wheelchair stopped dead in its tracks. I, on the other hand, continued to fly through the air like a wounded dock.

When I finally landed face down with a thud that sounded like an earthquake, Micki and the boys who were so scared. They rushed up to me and asked me if I was alright.

As I rolled over and sat up, I saw the fear in their eyes. So I calmly asked the boys to go and get some marbles from the car.

They thought I had received a head injury.

I laughed and said, "The people in the house that was located on the ridge above can see us. What better thing for them to watch than a mom and dad playing marbles in the valley with their boys. Okay.

Now I was uninjured and could laugh about it. It was time to get back into the chair. More fun to come.

After the laughing was over, Micki proceeded to the motel office to ask for assistance. She returned shortly with a desk clerk who spoke very little English.

Micki discussed how she wanted to form an arm cradle between the clerk and her, and he finally grasped her hands and arms. I placed my hands on each of their shoulders and pushed up while they placed their cradled arms beneath me.

As they started to pick me up, I looked straight in to the eyes of the foreign-speaking clerk and said, "Sir, this is the third time she has tried to kill me."

Immediately I felt his arms giving away. Micki meanwhile, is stuttering," He is kidding! He is kidding!"

I responded, "Look at the marks on my throat where she tried to kill me with a knife."

Again, his arms gave way.

With that, I began to laugh. He looked at me as if I had lost my mind.

Micki and he finally got me back into the chair. He then walked back toward the motel office with his head down and mumbling some foreign language.

Micki then started beating on me. "If you ever do anything like that again, I **will kill** you!" she threatened.

I couldn't stop laughing.

Can you imagine what that clerk told his wife about that day on the job?

* * *

The next day Micki and the boys took a tour of the Luray Caverns.

Our vacation continued over the Blue Ridge Parkway. The beautiful sites and animals we saw were great.

Micki and the boys loved the mountains. I, on the other hand, found them to be difficult to maneuver from a wheelchair.

After a week of vacation and sightseeing we headed for home.

* * *

They made sure the next vacation we took was to Niagara Falls.

We had the hell scared out of us when we went through customs at the US/Canadian border. The border agent stuck his head in the driver's side window and started asking questions while looking at everything inside the car.

I had never experienced anything like this in my life. I did not know what I had done wrong and had trouble answering his questions.

He could see I was confused about the whole ordeal. He saw the hand controls and wheelchair, smiled and said to go ahead.

I told Micki, "I didn't know I was going to take a lie detector test, just in order to see the falls."

We looked for a parking lot close to the falls area. As we pulled into a parking lot close by, I looked up to see a man standing in the middle of the lot directing traffic. I told Micki that the guy looked like Lester Lynch.

Following his directions, I pulled up and stopped. Placing my head out the driver side window, I asked if he were Lester.

He stopped and looked at me. Sure enough, the guy was Lester!

Micki and I both asked, "What are you doing here?"

We talked for some time about how far we had both come since the — accident. Lester will always have a burn mark on his hand from where he removed melted steel from my body that day.

We wished each other a safe and enjoyable trip and went our separate ways.

Micki, the boys and I spent two days observing the magic and beauty of the falls. We then traveled along the river through Canada to the next border crossing. Back in the USA we drove through Buffalo, New York and looked at as many sites as possible.

With no air conditioning in the car, two small boys and a wheelchair in the back seat, we decided to head for home. We arrived home safely, and everyone had a great time.

It was time to get back to work on my radio course with the N.R.I. and listen to the ham radio operators.

By this time we had outgrown our little bungalow, which wasn't handicapped accessible. So I had great difficulty in getting around it.

Micki found a house for sale on Clyde Ave., one street north of our present location. We both looked at the house and loved it.

Knowing that I was going back to work in January of 1970, I asked my mother for a loan to assist in the purchase of the house. She willingly assisted, and the purchase was made.

We finally had our own house—no more renting.

The insurance company paid to have a concrete wheelchair ramp to the front door and one in the garage. 111 Clyde Ave, Fruitland, Maryland was now our little heaven on earth. We had Thanksgiving in our new home, with all the family joining us.

* * *

Finally the day came when I received a call from Ray Landon, who said he wanted to come by and talk to me about my returning to work.

When he arrived, we had a short discussion about our vacation and the purchase of our home. Then came the good and bad news.

It seemed the only job available for me was junior clerk in the Salisbury District office.

Think about it: a lineman who handled nothing smaller than a 13/16 socket and ratchet now pushing a number two Ticonderoga pencil. It would surely break as I placed it in my hand.

I asked if there wasn't something I could do within the stations department line crew. Ray told me no that this was the only job available. He told me that if I wished, I could go on Social Security.

My heat sank. This meant I would reduce my paycheck from $135.00 a week to $50.00 per week. All I could think about was the loss of our little piece of heaven, our house.

Ray told me that this would just be a start. From there I could work my way up the ladder. The good news was I had a job.

Micki saw my deep concern. She told him, "Ed will take that junior clerk job and we will make out fine. But don't be surprised when you see Eddie climbing up that ladder in record time, he hasn't come this far to let a little thing like this set him back."

After getting myself together and hearing what Micki had just said, I thought that this was my opportunity to go back to work and show all the people who contributed with their prayers, money, and physical assistance that their investment was not wasted. It was an opportunity for someone who wanted to succeed. I wanted to make them glad they helped us.

The meeting ended on a good note and a schedule to return to work January 2, 1970.

Now the Christmas preparations in our now house were in full swing. Micki had, as usual, extended herself to the fullest in making the house beautiful for the holidays. The tree was all decorated with gaily wrapped presents under it, and two brand new bikes were hidden in the garage. The house was filled with the smell of freshly baked cookies and my favorite—peanut butter balls. I loved that holiday. We all enjoyed our gifts and the boys made my day interesting trying to get out of their way while they very wobbly rode their new bikes.

* * *

Finally the big moment came. January 2, 1970, was here and I was on my way back to work.

Thoughts bombarded my head as I drove to work. *How will the people react to me when they haven't seen me in a wheel chair?. How will I react to their reactions? How will I handle someone if they show me pity?*

I didn't want any pity….just opportunity. I wondered who this new boss of mine was…Mr. Sid Burtman. I knew he was the district Manager, but I wondered what he looked like and what kind of man he was.

All these questions would soon be answered.

I arrived in the company parking lot and transferred from my car into my wheelchair in front of a cheering group of friends. They all gathered around to welcome me back to work. This felt great. We started joking with each other as though nothing had ever happened.

They kept me company through the parking lot into the building, making sure there was nothing I needed, all the while painting a scary picture of my new boss, Sid Burtman.

After traveling up the ramp to the loading dock, I opened the door and started down the hallway toward the Salisbury District Engineering office. As I turned the corner and entered the office I was met my Ray Landon, who introduced me to Sidney (Sid) Burtman , Doug Boyce, the District engineer, Bob Lord, Press Wheatley and Bunky Austin, Engineering field personnel. These would be my fellow employees for the next six months as I worked as a junior clerk.

Then a position opened for engineer's helper or Field engineering personnel. I placed a bid on this job and got it. However being in a wheelchair, I could progress to the second step only out of five steps. It was said that I would remain at the second level for the rest of my time there… only because they had not dealt with anyone in a wheelchair, with my tenacity or stubbornness.

Did they think I would be satisfied? At least it was a pay increase.

Doug Boyce moved on to another engineering position and Ernie Mathews became our now district distribution engineer. After union representation by Bob Lord and my work effort, the freeze was lifted at the second step. The summer of 1973 found me in the middle of a field, driving stakes for underground cables installation.

One day as I sat with a lap full of stakes and a mallet, Bob drove up in his pickup and told me to get back to the office right away.

"Why?" I asked.

"Just do it," he ordered and left.

When I got back to the office, Ernie Matthews told me a woman had called him on the phone and gave him hell for having a man in a wheel chair out in the hot sun driving stakes in the ground.

I laughed and asked him why he didn't tell her that is what I wanted to do.

Ernie told me, "I tried to tell her that you are very capable of handling that chair. She then threatened to turn me and Delmarva Power over to any agency that would put us all in jail."

Ernie told me he had to give me another job where she wouldn't see me. But we all had a good laugh and I assured them they would not be going to jail...although it did sound tempting.

Eight years passed until the position of engineer fieldman opened in the office. I bid on it and received it. At least it was another pay increase.

I didn't mention that in June of 1970 I started taking college courses at night. This was at Delaware Technical and Community College in Georgetown, Delaware. I took technical math, Algebra, Trig, and Calculus....all with nothing but a slide rule.

I enjoyed the challenge of college life and continued with more courses after I finished these. I went to Salisbury University to take accounting. In March of 1970, I approached Ray Landon and asked him what it would take to advance in the company. (My main goal was that of System Operator. This is the toughest inside job within the company.)

He placed three large three ring binders in front of me. "Read these and then tell him if you have the right stuff."

I spent the better part of an hour going over the different pages then I gave them back to him and told him that someday I would be a System Operator. He just looked at me, smiled, and told me good luck. That was when I decided to take college courses in mechanical engineering and then financial accounting. This was all in the effort to stimulate my brain and prepare for the necessary testing to become a System Operator.

In 1978 an opening for assistance system operator was posted on the board. 28 people were selected to be tested. I was one of the 28.

It was required that we fly to Pittsburgh, Pennsylvania to be tested. This took place at a psychological service at Pittsburgh located at 1005 Penn Street, Pittsburgh.

It was decided that we would go in pairs. A gentleman by the name of Martin Mitchell and I were to go together.

Martin and I had both grown up in Sussex County, Delaware. He, in Milton, Delaware, and I, in Lewis. We lived only 18 miles apart but didn't know each other at that time. We found out that we had several friends in common from our home area.

We packed our clothes and I drove to B.W.I. Airport in Baltimore, Maryland. When we arrived, I took one look at the planes, knowing a DC10 had crashed recently and told Martin I was afraid of flying.

He promptly got in touch with management at the terminal and advised them of my concerns and that I was in a wheelchair. Soon two men called me into their office—one was black and one the other one white. They talked to me for several minutes about airplane safety and assured me I would not be flying on a D. C. 10.

They completed their talk by saying, "Now you have our assurance in both black and white."

I decided that I just might live through this, so Martin and I headed down to the loading chute. When we approached the door of the plane a C 111, I could see the wheelchair was too wide to go down the isle.

We backed out into the chute and allowed others to board the plane. Two men arrived with what looked to be a refrigerator cart. I looked at it and ask what that was for, at which time they told me it was a personal transport.

"In other words, we are going to transfer you from your chair to this seat, strap you in and take you into the plane. We will then transfer you to your seat," one of the men explained.

I looked at the 10-inch-square. "This will never work," I said. "I weigh 230 pounds and my butt is wider than that seat."

Against my better judgment, they proceeded to do just what they said they were going to do.

Our seats were just behind the front bulkhead on the port side. Martin was next to the window. We were belted in and going down the runway.

I could hear a rubbing sound and asked Martin," What is that noise?"

He paused for a moment. "I think the plane has a loose brake shoe."

I felt the sweat starting in my armpits

While we were parked on the runway awaiting permission to take off, Martin looked out the window. "Maybe we can get over them," he commented.

"Get over what?" I asked him.

"The two trucks parked on the runway ahead of us."

Now my hands are sweating.

We started down the runway and the rubbing sound turned into a bumping sound, increasing in frequency as we gained speed. All at once there was a rather loud sound of metal hitting together as we became airborne.

Martin looked at me and said, "I think we just lost our brake shoes." The next words out of his mouth were, "I don't know how we were going to land in Pittsburgh."

I had 10—I repeat 10—white knuckles and 10 fingers holding onto the armrest for dear life.

As we continued our climbed, he said, "The pilot has the pedal to the metal now, he sure is shifting those gears smoothly. Do you think will still be able to see the earth when he stops his climbing?"

By now I thought, *The hell with the test I want to go home.*

When we leveled off, Martin asked the steward just how high we were and how fast we were going. She replied, about 30,000 feet and 500 mph and that we would be in Pittsburgh in 28 minutes.

The flight went very smoothly until we got near Pittsburgh. The plane started to slow down; and Martin looked at me and said they must be testing their air brakes. "I sure hope they work, because I think we lost the brake shoes back at the other airport."

I could not say a word.

The plane banked in preparation for landing in Pittsburgh. Martin looked out the window and said he sure hoped the pilot could see them.

Again, I asked what *they* were.

He said, "It looks to me like there is a herd of deer on the runway."

As we started to descend, Martin said that if I heard several loud bumps, we might be eating venison for some time.

As we touched down, I, like a dummy, listened for any noise of any kind, but I heard nothing.

As we came to the stop at the terminal, Martin said he thought maybe that mechanic had replaced the brake shoes while we were in the air.

He looked at me and laughed. "You're saying that my first plane ride wasn't that bad, was it?"

I told him I thought the test now would be a breeze compared to traveling with him.

We left the plane only to get into a taxi driven by Mario Andretti, who scared the hell out of both of us on the way to the William Penn Hotel

* * *

The next day we both had eight hours of one test after another. The following day was filled interviews.

That afternoon - we went back to the airport for our return flight. Only this time, I had a beer to calm my nerves.

We each had great stories to tell our wives. He, on how he scared the hell out of me and I, on the other hand, told of how someday I would get even with him.

The selection process continued. During this time, Martin was offered the position of supervisor of maps and records and took that job. Now the remaining applicants were down to three. I was still in the running.

During the next few days, the supervisor of system operations had the three of us tour a local substation. We were given a thorough explanation of all the equipment then brought back to the building and tested again.

After the test I found out that there were two vacancies, and I had come in third. I was extremely disappointed. I was told I knew too much. I didn't understand at that time, but the answers would come.

I returned to my engineering fieldsman's position in the Salisbury division. Ken Ellers, the division engineer, was also very disappointed. He also felt the decision left a lot to be desired.

The next two years passed quickly. In late 1980, Martin Mitchell told me of a rumor that there would be a group formed to handle the distribution problems throughout Delaware Maryland and Virginia. This group would be in distribution engineering but work closely with system operators. This group would be management and not union.

I watched the board and listened for any news. And sure enough, the position for five distribution controllers was posted on the board.

I bid on one of these positions and although I had already been tested I didn't require any more. But I wanted to and did retest to prove myself.

I became one of the selected newly formed distribution controllers. In June of 1981 we five—Dennis Callahan, Larry Bonniwell, Bert Brittingham, Tyrone Ennals, and I—started a new function within Delmarva Power.

Since it was summer, we soon were dealing with one thunderstorm after another. This group became—and still is—a vital part in the restoration of the electric energy to all residential, commercial, and industrial customers on the peninsula. I am very proud I was a part of one of the first distribution controllers to sit at the radio console. And I am a T/6 paraplegic. Who would've guessed?

After several successful years as a distribution controller, this group was absorbed into system operations position. I haven't mentioned these jobs are swing shift. This means 7 to 3... 3 to 11, and 11 to 7 shifts.

I loved the nature of the work as well as the changing shifts. I worked hard to learn everything I could about the power plants/ generating plants/stations.

In 1990 a position for system operator opened. I was afraid to get my hopes up but put my name in anyway.

You can only imagine the celebration that went on at our house when I got the job. That year was a bountiful year—I got my dream job and we were blessed with the birth of our first grandson, Jordan, born Oct 5th 1990.

When news of my promotion was published in the company's weekly news magazine, I received a copy in my mail box. This copy was in an envelope. When I opened it I saw my promotion circled in ink and the words, *Congratulations! H. Ray Landon*, followed by *See you soon.*

Ray was now Executive Vice President of Delmarva Power now stationed in Wilmington, DE. He later came down to Salisbury to congratulate me in person.

It was a great moment. I had returned to work in a wheelchair in 1970 as a junior clerk and now I was a system operator.

Ray had followed my progress over the years. He and I were both proud of my accomplishments.

1990 was a very good year for our family. Micki and I were very happy with the results of our blood, sweat, and tears. On March 26, 1991, our family was again blessed with a grandchild; this time we got a beautiful little girl name, Lindsey Michelle. Micki "Michelle" Buck was very proud.

In 1993 I was honored by receiving the Governor's award for being the Outstanding Marylander of the year with a disability.

* * *

After I spent two more years as system operator, all system operators in Salisbury were to be moved to Christiana, DE to do all generation and transmission switching from that location. Our home is wheelchair accessible and since I was nearing retirement age, I requested to remain in Salisbury.

December 31, 1994 was my last day as a system operator. This was one of the saddest days of my life, as I had had a dream; over several years of hard work, I had achieved it and enjoyed every day I went to work.

Eventually, I learned why I had been turned down in 1978 for *knowing too much.* The department head at that time wanted an individual with little or minimal knowledge of electrical theory. I had become a ham operator WA3RFH (now WA3ED) and he thought that I would take longer to make a switching decision.

He didn't want an engineer. He wanted someone who could be trained with his approach in reacting quickly to the events at hand. I now understand his logic but respectfully disagree with his decision.

In January 2, 1995, I went to work as Supervisor of the newly formed drafting and records department in distribution engineering. It so happened this was the year for an early retirement program.

The supervisor of both the mapping department and capital property records department retired. Both departments were brought together, forming a drafting and record department.

I, having been a junior clerk, engineer helper, engineering fieldman, distribution controller and a system operator, had the qualifications to fill the supervisor position.

I now had the responsibility of ten employees in the department plus two to assist on separate projects on loan from two other project engineers. The challenge here was not that I didn't know the transmission and distribution system over three states—I knew them extremely well. The challenge was having the ability to communicate with all personnel in the department.

From 1995 through March 1, 1998, an outstanding team was created—a combination of man and women, black and white. They helped me learn to supervise a group of people by good communication skills rather than giving switching instructions over a radio or telephone.

The other highlight of 1995 was the birth of our third grandchild—another girl by the name of Emily...a beautiful blue eyed blonde born on November 12th.

On January 27, 1998, our last grandchild was born—Douglas Edward. Now I could feel my chest swell. This was also the year that Delmarva Power merged with Atlantic City Electric in New

Jersey. This new company, called Conectiv. 1998, also brought another early retirement opportunity.

My department was going to be moved in part of Wilmington. I was given the choice of going to Christiana, Delaware; Salem, New Jersey; or take an early retirement. Now 55 years of age with 71 days short of 33 years of service, 28 in a wheelchair, I decided to take the early retirement.

On March 1, 1998, I officially retired. My last day at work was a heart breaker. I was leaving the best family of friends a man could want. They covered all three states and not just one building.

Leaving the parking lot for the last time with the memories of my first day at work—May 10, 1965—and the men on the line crews.....
July 28, 1967—the day of the accident and the things which led to the electrocution....the years of recovery and the people who provided the opportunity for my success....the times I was in the different hospitals...Easton Hospital....Johns Hopkins in Baltimore....
Peninsula Regional in Salisbury....Children's Hospital in Baltimore...
to the Kenneth B. Norris Cancer Clinic at the University of Southern California. I had overcome all these challenges in 28 years of work from the seat of a wheelchair.

Our dreams have been accomplished, even though Micki suffered a heart attack on April 16, 1997, due in most part to stress. She has been by my side all the way. As I look back on all I have received and all we have accomplished, I know the true reason I have been *dying to survive.*

IN SUMMARY

I want to thank the supreme architect of the universe for my existence as well as Micki, my guardian angel, and our two sons, Dan and Rob. We have grown as a family and suffered much but with the suffering came strength and the ability to lean on one another. As I have mentioned we have been blessed with four grandchildren, Jordan, Lindsey, Emily and Douglas Edward. We now have the daughter we have always wanted, Laraine, our son Rob's wife. All these things make me so happy for what I have, that I don't have time to cry over what I don't have. I can say that I have faced the East and continued my journey through life with freedom, fervency and zeal. When the final chapter is written I can only say, THANK YOU GOD, THANK YOU FOR EVERYTHING.

Micki's Story

Ahhh to be 17 again...or maybe not. If I had known what lay ahead in just a few years, well.....

It was the summer of 1960 and I was working in my parents' shop..... Mezick's Gift Shop and Shell Garden. The shop was located in a resort town called Dewey Beach, about a mile south of Rehoboth Beach, Delaware, a much larger resort town then Dewey. It was early July, and I had my parents' car, doing the normal teenage thing.

I was going to Rehoboth to visit my aunt when I saw the gas gauge was low. I pulled into a gas station and the guy who came out took my breath away. I had dated quite a few guys from Lewes, the next town up, but had never seen this guy before. My first thought was *Where have you been all this time?*

As he washed my windshield, we made small talk. I batted my big brown eyes at him, hoping to get his attention. I just knew I would have to take a ride somewhere to burn up the gas so I could go back to the station to see this HUNK! It worked.

We started dating that July and had some great times together—snorkeling, going to the movies, stock car races, and just being together for a stroll on a moonlit beach.

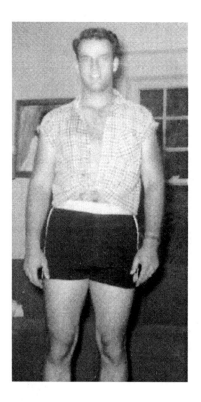

All too soon the summer was over. School started and with both of us involved in sports, we had a great time going to each other's games. He played football for Lewes High School and I was there to root him on. Then it was my turn. I played basketball for Lord Baltimore High School and he came to my games to root me on. It was a wonderful time of my life.

Somehow I knew that this was the guy I wanted to spend the rest of my life with. Everyone was against it, as far as family went. They thought we were too young, we didn't know what we wanted, and so forth. But we eloped after graduation and started our life together.

We moved seven times in the first three years, but always for a better job, more opportunity, a better future. Along the way we had two little boys three years apart. Dan was first, born in '62 and Rob was born in '65.

We were kids having kids, but God knew our time was running out and this was His plan. We were so happy with our little family.

We had moved into our little white bungalow in Fruitland Maryland in October of 64.

I was three months pregnant with our second son, Robbie, who was born April 28th.

Ed got a job with Delmarva Power, our local electric company, in May. Life was everything we could have asked for. We didn't have much money, but somehow we didn't know we were poor.

We lived in such a close-knit neighborhood. We all had children about the same age, so there was no lack of children running in and out of the house all day long.

Most of us were stay-at-home moms. Having a barbeque was a gathering; once the fire was lit, one after another, the neighbors would come over, some with meats and others with potato salad or other goodies. Soon we had a block party going. We felt very lucky to live where we were.

The next two years went by very fast. I couldn't believe we would soon be celebrating our 6th anniversary. We were so happy. All was right with the world.

In July of 1966, we took our first family vacation. We went to Lake Erie, where Ed and Danny went swimming while Robbie and I sat on shore with a bucket of water. Danny's eyes were so big, having never seen a lake with big waves. To see my big strong husband being so gentle with our little boy, making sure the waves didn't break on him made my heart swell.

We went on the Niagara Falls, ohhing and ahhing at the size of the falls and its beauty. We have such fond memories of that trip and we savor every minute of it. I am so thankful to have those memories. It was our first and last *normal* vacation.

* * *

I was out hanging diapers on the clothesline when I heard the phone ringing. It was 10:15 a.m. hurrying into the house, I told the boys to stay right by the back steps as they played with their little cars, making roads in the dirt. If only I had known that when I answered that phone, our lives would never be the same. I wonder if I would have answered it. To just prolong the inevitable.

* * *

The previous night Eddie and I lay in bed, making plans for our vacation that year. I always saved money weekly for the one-week vacation we would take with our children. Snuggling and giggling like children, we were having so much fun telling each other where we wanted to go and play-arguing over who would get their way.

The next morning when the alarm went off, Ed leaned over and told me not to get up. He was a linesman. I remember how elated we were when he got that job. It was one of those jobs young people just dream about-great benefits, good money, paid vacation. Sure, you lived week to week, but it was a steady job where there hadn't been a lay-off or strike in a very long time.

The boys were still sleeping. It was cool-good sleeping weather. I lay there with eyes only half open as he kissed me good-bye, said that he loved me and would see us at 5:15. I mumbled something like, "Love you. Have a good day. See you at dinner."

The phone was still ringing and when I reached it. A voice on the other end told me there had been an accident. Ed had been hurt.

My heart stopped. "What do you mean he's been hurt? What happened? Where is he? How badly is he hurt?" So many questions so little answers.

The voice of the safety director broke through my babbling. "Mrs. Buck, a car is on its way to get you to take you to the hospital. Ed is in Easton Hospital and we'll get you there as soon as possible."

I called my neighbor and told her that Ed had been hurt but that was all that I knew-something about he got shocked or something but that they were sending a car for me. (Her husband worked at the same company as Ed so they took turns driving. Today I had the car, so I wondered why they just didn't tell me to drive to the hospital; why were they coming to get me.)

Peggy Tarr came right over and took the boys with her. She had a daughter the same age as Danny, so it seemed natural for them to go to her house. And as our boy's Godmother, she was also my best friend who, unbeknown to me at that time, would be a lifeline with her humorous letters from home in the months to come.

Finally a car pulled up and Monroe Whaley, the president of the union, and Stuart Flannery, the safety director, got out. I ran up to them and asked them what was going on.

"Micki," they answered, "We need to get you to the hospital in Easton as soon as possible."

"But what happened," I asked. "How badly is he hurt?"

"All we know is that he came in contact with an energized power line and has been taken to Easton Hospital."

I grabbed my purse, closed the door, which was never locked, and got in the back seat of the car. This was in the days (1967) that you never locked your doors, but if you wanted to, you went to the hardware store, got a skeleton key, locked the door and left it under the mat. (Anyone could get a key, also. So we never bothered to get one and felt perfectly safe.)

* * *

In what seemed to take hours, we finally got to the hospital. I went into the emergency room and a nurse rushed up to meet me. I stared at her. *She was crying. Why?*

I asked her where Ed was and could I see him.

"Oh, I am so sorry. We waited for you as long as we could, but he had to be transferred to John's Hopkins Hospital." she answered.

My heart stopped. *Transferred? THE John's Hopkins Hospital, where they take very serious cases?* My mind was racing.

"How badly is he hurt?" I asked her.

With tears still in her eyes, she said, "Oh he is hurt pretty badly, but he's going to be fine." Then she hugged me.

My world was spinning. *If he is going to be all right, then why the tears? It didn't make sense.*

I knew I had to put one foot in front of the other, go out the door, and get into the car for the two-hour drive to Baltimore. *I WAS GOING TO JOHN'S HOPKINS HOSPITAL!*

Monroe asked me if I had any money.

I looked at him blankly. I was still in shock. "Ah, money?"

"Yes. You will need some money there," he answered.

I opened my purse. We didn't have the luxury of having much money. I was a stay at home mom, the one thing Ed insisted on.

We brought those two little boys into this world, and we will take care of them. We didn't know any people who had two cars, steak for dinner or who took cruises. Our life was simple -we had hot dog stew or a roast chicken that lasted for dinner and lunch for Ed. The boys, along with all the neighbor kids, would come to the back door and I would give them all popsicles made from a ten-cent pack of Kool Aid ®. Or I would get a big box of oatmeal and make cookies.

Every night at 5:15 Ed would pull into the driveway and the boys would run to meet him. They were always so excited to see Daddy. A boy in each arm, he would come into the back door with a smile on his face, no matter how tired he was.

Daddy, their daddy-so big, so handsome...6'1", 227lbs, 46-inch shoulders, 36-inch waist, dark brown hair and hazel eyes. I used to laugh, calling him my missing link between ape and man, without his shirt on; he looked like he was wearing a sweater.   Ah, the memories of his coming to bed and snuggling after he came out of the shower, with the smell of soap clinging to his chest. My heart still skips a beat when I think of those days.

* * *

Would we ever get to the hospital?

"Mrs. Buck?"

"Oh, please, call me Micki." I was only 24, and this gentleman who was a good ten years my senior, was being so formal. "What was your question?" I asked.

"Do you have any money?" He asked again.

"Oh, that's right. Let me look. I know I had a twenty-dollar bill left. Yes, here it is. I have twenty dollars," I said.

Mr. Whaley told Mr. Flannery to stop at the electric company just on the other side of Easton and he would get some money, in case I needed it. I just looked at them.

The nurse said that he had been hurt but that he would be all right. I didn't need any money. I would be going home with them and Ed would be coming home in a couple days. I would get the car and come back up to pick him up.

We stopped in Easton, anyway. I chomped at the bit to get going. Somewhere up the road an ambulance was taking the most important man in my life to the hospital. I wanted to be there now.

We finally got to the hospital. In the emergency room, I walked up to the person at the desk and asked to see Ed Buck.

"Are you his wife?" the lady asked.

"Yes, I am. I was told he was slightly hurt and I want to see him. Can I do it now?"

"Well, honey, they are getting him cleaned up at the moment so it will be just a couple minutes and then you can see him," she said.

Relief came over me. He was not hurt badly and I would get to see in soon.

I sat down with the two men and waited. As I sat there, Lester Lynch came around the corner. Both of his hands were bandaged. He was a fellow linesman with Ed.

"What happened?" I whispered.

"He was on fire, Micki, I had to put out the flames. I beat them out with my hands. I'm okay." He answered.

Small talk. Waiting. A cup of coffee. Waiting. More small talk. More waiting. Waiting . Waiting. Waiting.

The nurse came to me. "Mrs. Buck, the doctor wants to talk to you before you see your husband."

I looked at her with more questions racing through my mind. *Why the doctor? Why can't I just see Ed? There is something they aren't telling me.*

I followed her into the doctor's office. Funny, how you can remember the name of someone who impacts your life so greatly, even after 39 years.

Dr. Leand stood as I entered the room. We shook hands. He asked me to sit down, that he wanted to talk to me. I was silent.

"Mrs. Buck, we have a very sick man here. Do you know how badly he was injured?" he asked.

"Well, the nurse in Easton Hospital said that he had been hurt but that he would be fine. Why are you saying this?" I asked

He looked at me with sympathy in his eyes. I felt uneasy. Fear started running through me. I didn't want to listen to this man anymore. I just wanted to see Eddie...my Eddie.

Dr. Leand started talking, but I didn't want to hear what he was saying.

"Mrs. Buck, I am so sorry to have to tell you this, but I don't think he is going to make it," he said softly. "He took 69,000 volts of electricity three times. He has been burned over 80 percent of his body. Please don't get your hopes up. He isn't going to make it."

I got mad. *How dare he tell me Eddie wasn't going to make it. NO! NO! We were going to celebrate our 6th anniversary in 7 days. Of course, he was going to be there for that. We have two small boys who love their Daddy very much. Of course, he was going to be there to play baseball, fish-do all the things that Daddies do. Don't you dare tell me he is going to die!*

I could hear Dr. Leand's voice in the background, but my mind was fighting him. So soothingly he was telling me all these bad things while my mind was screaming for him to shut up.

In a trembling voice I asked him to give me a percent...something I could hold on to...just a small lifeline.

He told me 80/20.

I stared at this man who was ruining my life. "You mean 80 that he is going to die?"

"Mrs. Buck, I know this is hard on you but I don't want to see you get your hopes up only to have them dashed." He tried to be kind.

I composed myself and asked to see Eddie. He said he would take me, but first I had to know a couple of things..

By now I was ready to fall completely apart. All I wanted was to see Eddie, to have him tell me he was all right, to have him hold me, which was something I would not have for the next five months.

I could hear Dr. Leand talking to me, so again I brought myself back to reality.

"When people are burned as badly as your husband, they lose so much body fluids, their heads swell, their skin is raw...oozing. He is fully conscious and doesn't know how badly he is hurt. For his sake, you must *not* show *any* emotion. Keep it light. Don't let him know you are scared. Can you do this?" He asked. "I don't want you going into his room and falling apart or screaming. Now before you go in, you have to promise that you can do it."

OH, MY GOD...what is going to happen to our lives? Can I do it? Yes, I could do anything if it would help Eddie.

* * *

They took me up to Halsted two...room 217, a private room. They handed me a gown, mask and head cover. I had never seen these things before. But I put them on.

"Are you ready to see him? Are you alright?" the nurse asked me.

I looked at her name tag...Mrs. Dananski.

"Sure," I answered, "I can do this."

Slowly I opened the door. I saw someone in the bed. I walked over to it and said to the man, "Hi, baby," I said.

I may have gasped a little, but he didn't hear me, thank goodness.

He answered, "Hi, honey, guess I messed up this time. Looks like I'll be here for a few days."

I looked at this man. It was Eddie's voice coming out of someone else's body. I didn't recognize him. His head was the size of a basketball.

He was lying there with a contraption keeping the sheet off the burns. White cream covered his whole body.

My head was spinning. *Keep it light! Keep it light!* My mind was screaming. *But it isn't Eddie. Where is Eddie? Why is that Eddie's voice coming out of that...that...that stranger?*

"Are you alright, honey?" he asked.

"Yes, yes, I am fine. It was just a hurried trip, and I guess I am in a little shock. But, hey, this wasn't fair of you to take a vacation without us."

He laughed. "Where are the boys?"

I told him that Peggy had come over and taken them to her house. She had told me not to worry about them. They loved her and Mr. Bob, her husband. So they were in good hands.

I could touch his hand-only his right hand. The electricity had gone in his left hand and come out his right foot.

I stood there talking for about 3 minutes when the nurse came in and told me I would have to leave for a little bit while they worked on him. I remember the room seemed too stark—one hospital bed, a chair...just a fold up chair, a TV, a table laden with medical supplies, and a dresser, also with medical equipment on it.

I got to the door and looked back at Eddie. He couldn't see me, but there he was, lying there with tubes running from his body. He had 6 IVs running at one time. He was surrounded by IV poles and lines going in all direction.

As if sleepwalking, I left the room and stood in the hall. *This has to be a bad dream. I want to wake up. I want to wake up.*

The nurse came over and grabbed my arm. "Here sit down," she ordered. "I'm afraid you are going to faint."

I guess I was in shock. The room seemed too bright. The lights seemed to be glaring. Everyone was looking at me with sympathy. I just wanted to run...run and hide.

"No, I'm not going to faint. I've never fainted in my life. Oops, well, I guess I did faint once when I had a sun stroke," I babbled. "The last year of high school, my parents, sister, and I went to Florida...I fell asleep on the beach and when I woke up, I went to the canteen. And as I got to the window to order a cold drink, I passed out."

What am I doing? Why am I telling them this? This is stupid. Get a grip on yourself. It will be all right, if you stay in control. They said don't show emotion...and you didn't. So you are in control.

"Look," I said, "I am fine. If I could just have a drink of water and sit for a minute, I'll be ok. I really want to know about Ed—his head, the bandages, the I.V.... I have never seen anything like that, and if I am allowed to be with him, I need to know everything."

Somehow, my inner strength was taking over.

"He has burns over 80% of his body. There is a plus and a minus to that," she patiently explained. "From what I understand happened, he was up a steel structure in a substation and when he went to throw the rope around the steel, it came in contact with a lightening arrester. The rope was wet and dirty, so the electricity went down the rope into his left hand came out at his arm pit, went across his shoulders back in his body down his leg and out his right foot. The breaker closed when it hit him and then opened again giving him another shot and then closed for the third time, hitting him again. Then it closed for good.

"He had his left foot looped around the steel with his body belt securely fixed. When the electricity hit him, he fell backwards and his clothes caught on fire.

"Another linesman climbed the steel and beat out the flames. (*Yes, Gene Shirk.... I know.*) The body belt kept him attached to the steel, but when his co-worker climbed the steel, they saw that he was not breathing.

"One of the linemen removed a piece of melting steel from his chest and burned his hands, also. (Yes, I know…it was Lester Lynch…he will carry that scar for life.) He yelled down to the other men that Ed was dead.

"Hooking a rope to the S ring on the body belt, he lowered him. However the S ring straightened out about three feet from the ground and the rope slipped out. Ed fell to the ground , and that jolted his heart to start beating again

"Your husband got up and started running. They grabbed him but in the meantime, someone had called for an ambulance. They held him on the ground 'til it arrived."

I stared at her, trying to take it all in. "You said there was a plus. Did I miss it?" I asked.

"When he fell over backwards the fire burned upward. With his head lowered, he did not breathe in any fire. So his lungs were spared," she replied.

"So much of his skin was blackened by the fire. And there are so many IV's. His head is so swollen….but he seems to know everything that is going on around him," I said.

"Well, to be honest, I don't want him to know how badly burned he is. The head swelling will go down in a day or two. The skin will be scrubbed off with a special soap...when you are burned, your body loses so much fluid and protein that not only are we replacing it in the I.V. but infection is attacking most of his body. So we have to keep pumping antibiotics in to try to keep ahead of it.

"Not only does he have the 6 IV's, but he gets 8 shots every four hours. We are doing our best to make this man live. And you have an important job to do," she explained.

"Me? What can I do?" I asked. Had she said I had to walk to the moon to make him live, I would have started that very minute.

"You are his reality. You will keep his feet on the ground...his morale up... give him a reason to keep fighting. It is very important for you to be here every day," she said.

Before Mr. Flannery and Mr. Monroe left, they took me aside. "We don't want you to worry about staying up here," they said.

They knew that we were just starting out. Ed had worked for them for two years and two months. And they knew that we had two small children, so money was tight.

"The union will pay for your hotel bill as long as we can. We don't know the length of his stay, but for the next month, you don't worry about hotel expenses."

Wow, I hadn't even thought that far ahead. I didn't know Baltimore... John's Hopkins...I had no clothes and only had $20.00 plus the $50.00 they had given my. But I knew I couldn't leave Eddie.

* * *

While I was in the emergency room waiting for them to get Eddie cleaned up so I could see him, I was paged over the intercom.

My heart stopped. I just knew they wanted to tell me he had died.

But it was my sister, Dee.

When I answered the phone, I said, "Dee, Ed has been badly hurt."

"I know," she replied, "I heard it on the news."

"The news?" I said in surprise.

"Where were you when it happened?" she asked.

I told her I was hanging up diapers on the clothesline. And I asked again about the story being on the news.

She told me the accident had happened at 10:00. And it was on the television at 10:15, just after it happened.

"If you had been in the house, you would have heard it there before they called you," she said.

Thank you, God, for not letting me hear it that way, I thought.

I told her that they weren't giving me any hope. That they were telling me he was going to die.

"Mick, what can I do for you?" she asked.

In the meantime, I had called Peg to check on the boys and she said they could stay with her for a few days until I got things sorted out. So I told Dee that I was staying in a motel across the street from the hospital but that I had no clothes or money.

She said she would be on her way in a little bit. She'd go to our house to pick up some clothes for me, get our vacation fund from the bedroom and bring everything up.

She stayed with me for three days, until she had to go home for a doctor's appointment.

I was holding up. I was not going to cry, I reasoned. If I cried, he would die. So that was my crutch—no emotion, no tears.

After the birth of her daughter, Lori Ann (Beth), Dee took on the responsibility of two more children. Danny and Robbie went to live with her and Mark, her husband, along with their son, Jeff, and a new baby daughter. I don't know what I would have done without my sister to count on.

* * *

My life took on a schedule of its own. For the next three weeks, I would leave the motel at 8 AM, walk over to the hospital, stay with Eddie until 5 or 6 PM and then go back to the motel, grab a bite and wait until morning to do it all again.

It was almost a blur—doctors coming in and out of his room...the many, many skin grafts...taking him to a room where he was lifted with the stretcher into what was called a Hubbard Tank. I would sit outside of the door and, as they took brushes and scrubbed and cut the dead skin back to the live skin, I would hear him screaming.... over and over. I couldn't bear to hear him in so much pain.

I begged the doctor to give him more pain killers. Dr Jabaley told me, "We have given him enough to knock out an elephant. We can't give him any more. We would kill him."

I would just sit there and cry. How long could he take this?

* * *

We had one special doctor. His name was Dr. Imas—my pessimistic Dr. Imas. He was a very caring doctor...always wanting me to face what he thought was the future.

"Don't get your hopes up, Micki," he warned me. "Pneumonia will probably set in. The infection he has is so bad. I don't know how much more his heart can take." And so on and so on and so on.

* * *

At first the only way I knew how to get into the hospital was through the emergency room. I was soon told that was not the way for me to get in. There were too many chances of my being followed home or watched…or even attacked. My newfound friends instructed me that I was to walk one block in each direction and no more by myself. I was to wait for one of the doctors who lived next door to the motel in the "550 Building" to walk me home if it was dark when I left the hospital. The nurses would call one of them who was going off duty. I felt very protected.

There were moments of lightheartedness. To keep Eddie's kidneys very active' the doctors ordered that he have three beers a day. Although at one time he enjoyed a cold beer, pretty soon it tasted like medicine to him. But some of the young interns would come into the room, hold a lighter under their hands and say, "I'm a burn patient. Can I have a beer?"

The doctors were very alarmed about the weight Eddie was losing and encouraged him to eat anything he wanted. When the people from home heard, they started bring up baked goods. His room looked like a bakery there were so many cakes, cookies of all kinds, brownies, pies. Our extended family couldn't do enough. Soon word spread of Buck's Bakery. There again, the interns, nurses, orderly and everyone knew that they were welcome to homemade goodies.

Never knowing what the day would bring was always nerve-wracking. I would go to the hospital and we would get Eddie up and into a chair to sit for a while.

Dr. Jabaley was the head of plastic surgery and ‐ in charge of Eddie's case. A very straightforward doctor, he told us up front ‐ how things would be. He never spared me the truth, which was how I wanted it.

He was going to be gone for a week – taking his family on vacation to Williamsburg VA, but he would keep in touch with the hospital while he was gone.

A young doctor came in the next day and gave Eddie a tetanus shot to ward off lock jaw as we didn't know when he had had his last shot. This was totally against Dr. Jabaley's orders but he was not there and I never saw that doctor again.

A couple days later, Eddie couldn't lift his foot right, he said it seemed very heavy. I told him he was just being lazy.

As the day progressed, the numb feeling went up his leg. By the fourth day he couldn't get out of bed. He couldn't move his legs. Then it went higher; soon he couldn't move his arms and breathing became difficult.

His nurse, Clara Hammie, got very concerned. She called for the doctors and then prepared a tracheotomy crash cart for incursion.

Slowly the numbing resided. He could breath and move his arms. However, He still could not feel or move anything below his waist.

He had become a T6 paraplegic.

* * *

I had a spiritual moment two days later, that was and is very special to me. In fact, it changed my life.

When I arrived at the hospital that morning, I walked in the front door and went around a statue of Jesus. He stood there with his arms outstretched. At times he looked like He was staring at me. I felt very comforted by the presence of that statue.

Now I was not a very religious person. Oh, I had gone to church as a child. My mother was the choir director and I sang in the junior choir. But in my teens, I drifted away. But I have to tell you about an experience I had with that statue and you can judge for yourself.

After a very bad night of sleeping (nightmares and being so very scared... every time the phone rang, my heart skipped a beat), I stopped in front of that statue and looked up at Jesus' face.

He looked so peaceful and calm. I stood there and prayed. I didn't pray for Him to make Eddie walk or be perfect; I asked that if it were in God's plan, would He just let - Eddie go home. Would he let him live...just let him live? So I could have my sweet husband and our two little boys could have their daddy?

Suddenly I felt like....well, the only way I can explain it was that it felt like a bucket of warm water was poured over my head and ran all the way down my body. I felt at peace. From that moment on, I knew he would be coming home...I didn't know when, how or in what shape he would be, but he was coming home.

His wonderful doctors still tried to prepare me for what they thought was going to happen, but I assured them that was not the case...he *was* going to live and he *was* going home with me.

However it was not smooth sailing from then on. There were still rough days to face. The paralysis had been a big scare and it was still such a shock.

When I entered the room a few days later, Dr. Jabaley stood at the head of Eddie's bed, looking sad and rubbing Eddie's forehead. He hadn't been there when the problem started and he was blaming himself.

Eddie was trying to reassure him that it was not his fault—that we understood there would have been nothing he could have done to stop it. We were very hopeful that it would be temporary. That was all we could do but hope.

They weren't sure what caused the paralysis called *Transverse Militias*. We have our own thoughts, as Ed describes. All we could do was wait to see what happened. There were other concerns. He was critical and would remain so for the next four months.

The doctors were very concerned about the weight Eddie was losing. They were giving him anything in the world he wanted to eat. So a week or so later, when he said he wanted something (which at this moment I can't remember), I walked down to a grocery store and bought it, along with a few goodies I thought he might eat.

As I walked down the hall toward his room, doctors and nurses were running out. I almost dropped the bag and hurried to the door.

Dr. Jabaley walked from the room. He was covered in blood.

My heart stopped.

I later found out they had called him out of the operating room. The blood on his scrubs was from someone else. ⁻

The news was bad. Eddie has lapsed into a coma. The foot where the electricity had exited was dead and needed to be amputated.

"Sign the paper, Micki. It has to be done," the doctor said.

"Oh, My God! I have to sign papers to cut off his foot?" I cried.

"He will die if you don't. The poison has already started attacking his body. We don't have much time. I'll give you five minutes."

I went into the room and stood at the end of his bed. I rubbed the foot good bye. THE foot that had kicked so many field goals…. THE foot that had run so many yards during football….

The foot that carried him as he chased me and catching me…tossed me up in the air only to be caught and hugged. *The* foot that the boys would stand on and walk all around the house, just like daddy.

Tears streamed down my face as I signed those papers.

Then they wheeled him away.

I kept reassuring my self that *when,* not *if,* the paralyzes left…. he would get an artificial foot and be just fine.

* * *

It wasn't long until the union told me they could no longer pay for the motel. This was going to be a long, drawn-out procedure. They would give me a few days to find somewhere else to live.

I felt so alone. No one was there with me. My sister, who had given birth to my niece, was trying to take care of our children. My parents were running their summertime business. And Eddie's mother was 66. I didn't know what I was going to do.

Dr. Jabaley (or Mike to me by now) and his wife, Mary, invited me down to the "complex" where most of the doctors who were residents of Hopkins lived. I told them of my dilemma and Mike said he would call his old landlady who had an apartment just two blocks from the hospital. If it were vacant, it would be perfect for me.

At the hospital the next day, Mary told me it was vacant and she would take me there.

I didn't know what to do. Here we had the little bungalow in Fruitland that I didn't want to give up, but how was I going to pay rent on this furnished three-room apartment and still keep the house?

Thank goodness, I had our vacation money. That would sustain me for a month.

I would go to the store and buy hotdogs, three potatoes and two cans of string beans, with one can of spaghetti sauce. I'd mix them all together and have hotdog stew for a few days.

However I had underestimated his fellow workers. Somehow they had figured we were struggling with finances.

Being very protective of Eddie, I didn't allow very many visitors. I didn't want to take the chance of someone bringing in some germs.

However, one day Gene Shirk and Lester Lynch, the two lineman who helped save his life came to see him and when they came into the room, they laid a watch box on Eddie's chest. At the time I thought it was so thoughtful, because his watch had been burned off, and I didn't know where it was.

Eddie couldn't open the box, as his hands were all bandaged. So I opened the box, expecting to see a watch fall out.

Instead, a roll of bills came out—enough money for me to pay the rent for a month and get a phone in case the hospital needed me (Those were the days long before any cell phone.)

If it weren't for those wonderful people, I wouldn't have been able to stay near Eddie. Every time I knew I couldn't pay the rent and would have to go back to Fruitland, someone would come up and give us money.

I would tell Eddie that I had enough to stay just two more weeks, and then I'd have to leave. He would get so upset. I tried every way to cut corners but knew my time was running out. Then there they would be, making it possible for me to stay. I will never be able to thank them enough.

I actually got to stay in Baltimore with Eddie until the day we both went home.

* * *

Now I could go get our boys and the car. And, if Eddie's mother would help me, we could be as close to a family as possible.

I took the bus back to Fruitland after explaining my plan to Eddie. He looked so scared; he didn't want me to leave him…I was his life line.

I promised to be back the next evening and hurriedly left for the bus station.

My best friend, Peg, met me at the Fruitland bus station and drove me to the house.

It was summer and the windows had been closed; humidity had caused water retention in the carpet. Our wonderful neighbors had gotten dehumidifiers and run them day and night until it was dry. Then they had cleaned out the refrigerator and left the door open.

The house looked so empty—no children's laughter as they rolled around on the floor, climbing all over daddy; no smells of dinner cooking—just silence, horrible silence.

When I walked inside, I did one thing that had bothered me since July 27th. I went to our bedroom to the closet to try to figure out what he had worn that day. I was so mad at myself for not getting up that morning, fixing his breakfast, going to the door and giving him an extra hug before he left. Then I would have known what he had on.

I saw that one of my favorite plaid shirts was missing. He had been wearing that plaid shirt and navy slacks. Oh, he looked so good in that outfit.

I remember sitting on the bed and hugging his pillow smelling him. I knew our lives would never be the same.

* * *

I got some things to take back to Baltimore for the children—clothes, toys, books, blankets, sleeping bags and pillows… and whatever else I could think of that might make that tiny apartment home.

I drove to Ocean View to get our boys. My heart still aches when I think of going to the crib to get Robbie, who was 2 ½, and he pulled away from me and wanted his grandmother. It would take a few days for him to know that I was Mommy and how much I loved him.

Then we went to get Eddie's mother, who was going to watch the children while I was at the hospital, then we would alternate. She would go to the hospital and I would take the children to a park or on some type of outing. The doctors kept telling me how important it was for a family member to be present.

This worked for about a week and then it was obvious that it was too much for Eddie's mother to do. Tensions were running high. Taking care of two small boys was more then she could handle. To be perfectly honest, I'm not sure I could do it.

I went to the hospital and listened to Eddie scream in pain and did my best to comfort him and to be his moral support. Then I went back to the apartment, only to hear Mrs. Buck fussing with me that at her age she didn't need this.

I told her that if she wanted to be the one to go to the hospital every day that would be okay. I would just take care of the children.

That wasn't possible, either, as she could not take the screaming and seeing her son in so much pain.

My back was against the wall. My world was crumbling. I was on the verge of a nervous breakdown.

They saw it at the hospital. I was wearing a size 16 when the accident happened July 27, and now it was the middle of August, and I was in a 10. I couldn't eat or sleep. When I wasn't at the hospital, I was waiting for that dreaded call, telling me he had died. And when I was with him, I was worried that the boys were getting on his mother's nerves. Yet I couldn't cry with the frustration. No!.....no!... that was my crutch. I couldn't give in to that.

Finally Mike asked me to see a psychiatrist. I looked at him in amazement.

"A psychiatrist?" I questioned. "I am not crazy! Why in the world would I see a psychiatrist?"

He explained that no one who is healthy would lose 22 pound as quickly as I had. I looked tired all the time. My nerves were at a breaking point. And I showed no emotions.

I couldn't tell him about my secret vow—NO EMOTIONS!

Okay, so I would go see the psychiatrist, Dr. Tony Reading. But it was a waste of time. I was fine just the way I was. I had a job to do, and I could do it. *I could do it.* As the little train said as he climbed the mountain, "I think I can.... I think I can."

* * *

As I sat down in the chair opposite of Dr. Reading, he was doodling something on a piece of paper.

Strange man, I thought.

Finally he looked up, "Hello, Mrs. Buck. How are you doing?" he asked.

Well I certainly was not going to tell this man all of my troubles. I would handle them myself. In actuality, I didn't know how or what I was going to do.

He turned the paper that he had been doodling on around for me to look at.

"Do you know what this is?" he asked.

I looked at him stupidly. *Duh...do I look like an idiot?*

"Okay, is this a game? It is a hot water tank." I replied. "Good drawing."

"Right," he answered. "Now what is this?" He was pointing to a little object on the bottom of the tank.

That is a pressure escape valve," I replied. By now I was not in the mood for his little games.

"Where is yours?" he very pointedly asked.

I stared at him dumbfounded. What the heck did he mean?

"Where is yours?" he repeated.

"Ahh... I'm not sure I know what you mean." I said.

"Your husband is critically injured, you are under tremendous strain with your family, and you are losing weight like mad. Your body language tells me you are as tight as a drum—ready to snap. And all I asked is where is your escape valve? Have you had a good cry?"

"No, I can't." I said.

"What? You can't cry?" he asked.

"No," I answered him honestly. "If I cry, he will die. I can't let that happen. I can't lose him. He is my life. I can't cry." I was almost hysterical.

"Do you really think you have that power?" Dr. Reading asked. "A crutch is not a bad thing to have...unless it destroys you. How can you be of any help to your husband if you aren't here? Do you realize that your body and mind are at a breaking point? You can't do anyone any good if you are gone."

I could feel my emotions boiling....going to erupt. *Fight this,* my mind was saying. *Don't give in.* But the more he talked so soothingly, the more I could feel I was losing.

I felt a tear running down my cheek. Soon there were two, then three. Finally the dam burst and I sobbed out all my fears, frustrations, and worries.

Dr. Reading was pleased that the emotions were working again.

* * *

I went back to Eddie's room and Hammie.

Ahh, Hammie. Let me introduce you to Hammie. I mentioned her before, but you have to know her better.

After about a week in the hospital with different private duty nurses, Ed was assigned a nurse by the name of Clara Hammie, a no-nonsense private duty nurse who knew her job better than anyone. The doctor would look to her for solutions to problems.

She was a gem. But there was just one problem: she was black. Not for me...when Eddie was a child of about 9, a gang of black boys had beaten him up to steal his new bike. He had a phobia about it.

And now his life was in the hands of a black woman. The biggest problem, as he told me when she left the room, was that he felt she was wonderful and he was so scared that he would say something to hurt her feelings. With the medicines he was on and losing the body fluids he did, he would sometimes hallucinate and say things he wouldn't remember.

"What if I say something to hurt her feelings, Mick?" he asked.

He was afraid to go to sleep for fear of blurting something out. We had to be up front with her. But he was going through so much; I felt it would be better for me to lay the cards on the table.

When she came back into the room, I asked her if she would have lunch with me. Puzzled, she agreed.

When we got to the cafeteria and sat down with our food, I explained the situation. I told her how much he felt for her and what his fear was.

She was so wonderful. She took this information and said for me not to worry; she would handle it. She was so amazing.

A couple of days later, I walked into the room only to hear her saying, "Mr. Buck if you don't turn over, I am going to smack your white ass."

As he burst into laughter, I entered his room. Their expressions were akin to catching children with their hands in a cookie jar.

She winked at me. All was right in this room.

She was my rock, never sugar coating things; teaching me how to care for him and making me feel useful. I didn't just sit in a chair watching; she taught me sterile techniques, and I assisted in his care. But she was not only my mentor but also my friend.

She saw my situation and knew it couldn't go on. She was the one who talked to Dr. Jabaley about what was going on and had him make the appointment with Dr. Reading.

When I got back to the room she was waiting.

"Are you going to face the truth now?" she asked.

"I'm doing alright," I answered stubbornly.

But that day with Dr. Reading made me realize I was not going to be able to control everyone's life.

I sat down in my chair; she could tell I had been crying. She came up to me and put her arms around me.

"It's time, Micki. You have to do it now."

I knew what she meant. I didn't want to face it, but I had to.

Later she remarried and became Clara Leake, but to us she was and always will be Hammie. Our Hammie!

I had to face the situation with our children, Danny and Robbie, my wonderful little boys who made the end of the day at the hospital bearable. I could come back to them, play with them, fix their dinner, tuck them into bed and read them a story. I'd then kiss them good night and be able to see them in the morning.

I had missed them so very much. And now they would be gone again. I was so angry, hurt, frustrated. I couldn't "fix" everything.

While my emotions were exposed, I had to make the phone call. I called my Mother and Father.

I knew they still had the shop open and were very busy. My sister had her baby girl and a five-year-old son to take care of. But my back was against the wall.

As soon as my mother answered, I broke down. "Mom, I can't do it alone any more. I need your help. Please, can you take the boys? I know I am asking a huge favor, but I don't know where else to turn."

I explained that is was too much for Eddie's mother, she just wasn't going to work with me..... there was no way out. I was so angry at his mother for putting up another barrier for me to try to cross....I was mad at life in general. I didn't want to give up. But I had lost control of the situation and now my back was to the wall and I was losing.

I am ashamed of how I acted in these next few hours, but once the emotions were allowed to escape, I'm afraid they did their own thing.

Mom said to bring them to their house and that they would do their best to take care of them. I went back to the apartment only to have Mrs. Buck start in on me about how difficult it was to take care of these boys...that they were making too much noise playing, she was too old to put up with this, she had enough to deal with, her son was in critical condition, and on and on she went.

Well, they—being Dr. Jabaley, Hammie, and Dr. Reading— asked for it. They wanted emotions, and I'm afraid I unleashed a crazy woman.

I have to say again, I am ashamed of myself for striking out because I was so hurt and letting emotions take over common sense. But I said to Mrs. Buck (that was what she told me to call her), "Get your stuff together and get your ass in the car. I am taking you back to Lewes, and I don't care if I ever see you again. I am trying my best to take care of *your* son and *your* grandchildren, and all you can think about is how hard this is on you."

I was on a roll. "How dare you put yourself first before Eddie? He is going through hell every minute of the day. I am the one watching him suffer and hearing his pain, and all I ask of you is to watch the boys so I am able to be there for him. Do you really think I enjoy it? Do you think I am having fun? You can't go to the hospital. You can't take care of his sons. You, you, you that's all you are thinking of...you !"

Oh, Dr. Reading, what have you done? You have turned loose a monster.

She went to the bedroom and packed her suitcase, (we only had the one bedroom and the boys and I slept on the couch and in sleeping bags on the floor beside me. But at least we were together...or had been.) Now they were going to be leaving me. Without a word, she went downstairs to the car.

I must say that was the quietest ride anyone has every taken— three hours of silence broken only by Dan's and Rob's quiet chatter in the back seat. They sensed there was a problem but were too young to understand.

Upon arriving in Lewes, she got out of the car and without a backwards glance went into the house.

I felt so bad. But at the same time I was so mad. Pride made me drive out of that driveway and yet I should have tried to talk to her to reason with her and make her understand. But no, anger made me go and not look back.

I got to my parents' house and with a very heavy heart, I had to say goodbye to our babies again. Thanks to you Dr Reading, I cried all the way back to Baltimore. I knew in my heart I didn't have any choice, but I hated it, all the same.

I got back late and just went to bed. The next morning when I got to the hospital, I was shaking. *Just nerves* I reasoned, having gone though a rough time.

Hammie took one look at me and told me to sit down. "I want to take your temp," she said.

Alarmed she told me it was 95, which was not good, and that I was to go to the nearest market, buy a big steak, go home eat all of it and go to bed. (As I have shared, she was my rock, friend, confidant and teacher. We laughed together, cried together and even sometimes fought.) She wanted me to take a day to just do something for myself—skip coming to the hospital, relax, go shopping…do something for enjoyment. But my only enjoyment was to be there watching him breathe…getting another day under our belts.

She was worried that I would burn out. She knew what lay in front of me. And having seen it many times before, she felt that I was too young to handle the responsibility of a paraplegic.

She had seen young marriages break up with the stress of having small children and a husband who needed a full time nurse for quite a while.

So we did have some "arguments" about that. She soon found out that I am such a stubborn person; I sometimes drive people to distraction. Once my mind is made up, what can I say? Hell or high water would not change my mind! Sometimes that's good and sometimes it is an awful burden. I have to prove I am right and sometimes it is only in my eyes that I am.

Weeks turned into months. Slowly but surely Eddie got better. After four months, we were told that he was being moved from his private room to a semi-private room. We were losing Hammie.

Our world was turned upside down again.

I went to Dr. Jabaley and very angrily told him how unhappy I was with this turn of events. Eddie needed Hammie, his room. Everything had gone so well, and now they wanted to change.

But Dr. Jabaley told me that Eddie was no longer critical and although we had a very long road in front of us, he couldn't justify to the insurance company the expense of a private duty nurse and a private room. So it was done.

My parents called me every three days so that I could talk to Dan and Rob, God, how I missed them. Many, many nights I would look at their pictures and cry. I would dream of our being a family and doing different things, only to wake up in the morning all alone.

Winter was coming on full force. Dr. Jabaley told me we might be able to go home for Thanksgiving.

I was so excited I made plans for a Thanksgiving dinner. Even if it was just in my head, it gave me something positive to plan for.

Unfortunately we had our Thanksgiving dinner in the hospital. But it was not all bad. Mom and Dad brought the boys to the hospital and, at this point, Eddie was looking more like himself...sure, he still had a couple IVs and was very thin, but he looked so good. (He always was a very handsome guy, and the student nurse would fight as to who would get to take him for test or x-rays.)

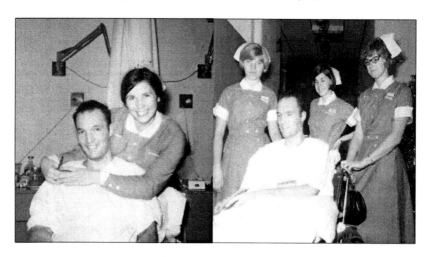

It was a joyous day. The boys were so happy to see their daddy, and all he wanted to do was cry. He was so excited at the prospect of seeing his little boys. He was always so protective of his two sons; as soon as he would come in the door from work, Danny and Robbie would run to him and he would pick up each boy in an arm, swinging them around laughing. It was the highlight of their day.

Ed is a wonderful father. There are stories I could tell about how protective he was…like when he changed Danny's diaper and put his fist in it so it wouldn't be too tight; and when I picked him up the diaper fell off. And one time when I was out hanging up clothes, he was watching Danny and the little walker broke. Danny was falling to the hard floor and Eddie was out of the chair and had his head cradled before he could hit the hard floor. And the time Robbie got Scarletina and Eddie yelled at the doctor for suggesting something as stupid as an alcohol bath. (I had to call the doctor back and tell him Eddie thought he meant whisky. The doctor had a good laugh. He knew Eddie was so scared for his baby. Rob was only about 4 months old.)

By this time Eddie was getting up in the wheel chair every day—but not being strong enough to push himself. I would take him all over the hospital to give him a change of scenery. The nurses would still come to take blood two or three times a day.

Eddie was so tired of needles that one day as we were waiting for the elevator to take us downstairs, a nurse got off and looked at Ed. "Mr. Buck?" she asked.

"No, he is in room 217," he answered.

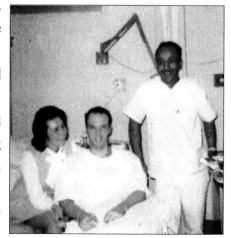

"Thank you," she said and down the hall she went.

The elevator door opened and he started wheeling himself. "Quick, hon, push me."

I did. Needless to say, he didn't have any blood drawn that day. He hid out, eating in the cafeteria, missing his medicine but enjoying himself more then he had in a long, long time.

So Thanksgiving Day was very special that year. Even though we couldn't be home, we were all together.

* * *

The first of December, the student nurses decorated his bed with mistletoe so they could give him a kiss. He really enjoyed that... actually more than I did!

Dr. Jabaley said we could go home before the holidays.

We would be home for Christmas! We were so excited.

I had plans to make. I would pack up my things from the apartment, take the car home and ride the bus back. I would only keep a few days' worth of clothes. We would have an ambulance take Eddie home, and I would ride in it with him.

Happily I headed for Fruitland. Our little bungalow looked so good now that I knew we were all coming home to it.

After I unpacked my things, I looked in the freezer and saw that I had a package of pork chops and that was all. But that was okay. I would slip to the store when we got home. I was too excited at the prospect of being together for Christmas.

Presents! What was I going to do about presents? I would figure something out...get a tree...shop for a few presents for the boys. Santa had to come for them.

* * *

I was ready to go back to Baltimore and prepare for the trip home in a few days.

Peggy took me to the bus station and as we started out, it was snowing. It came down heavier and heavier, but I had to get to Baltimore. I had promised Eddie I would be there that night.

I got on the bus and we left for the city. Eight hours later, we pulled into the bus terminal— a usual three-hour trip.

Exhausted, I had to walk to get a cab; none were to be found. Everyone was looking for a cab and by the time I got one and it took me to Washington Street where my apartment was, I was cold, wet and tired.

I called the nurse's station to ask them to please tell Eddie I was back and all right. I knew that if he looked out the window and saw all that snow, he would be worried sick.

Finally mid-December came, and Dr. Jabaley said it was all set for us to go home. But it was just going to be for Christmas; Ed had to be back in early January.

I would have agreed to anything, as long as we could spend Christmas with our children.

We said our tearful good byes to the doctors and nurses who, by now, were more like family than professionals.

Hammie was there and, with tears in her eyes, although she said she had promised herself many years ago that she would not let herself get close to a patient.

Right! So much for that promise! She was family.

Dr. Jabaley had tears in his eyes. When you see someone every day and then turn him loose, it is like losing a little part of your self.

We all cried that day—happy to be going home and yet not happy about losing the comfort of having Dr. Jabaley and Hammie close by in case something went wrong. We had depended on them for so long.

* * *

The ride home is the ambulance was memorable. When we stopped at a McDonald's for a sandwich, people walked by and looked in the door. Seeing a guy on a stretcher waving to them was hilarious. We were joking that no matter your condition, you can always take time for a Big Mac®.

I told Eddie that I knew we had a package of pork chops in the freezer, but the refrigerator was empty and the cupboards were bare. We laughed about it. We would eat peanut butter and jelly. Of course, I had to get the peanut butter and jelly…and bread.

* * *

As we turned down Hayward Ave—home, we saw something in our yard. On one of the two maple trees in the front yard was a big sign: *Yup ED, this is it…HOME SWEET HOME, and on the other… WELCOME HOME.* And at the front door was a very sturdy ramp that we later learned the guys from the electric company built.

The front door was open and there were neighbors inside. The ambulance crew got the stretcher out and took Eddie up the ramp into the living room.

To our amazement there was a hospital bed set up in the living room and the table laden with fried chicken and all the fixings. I just stood there staring.

Jeannie Pope lived on the other side of our driveway with her three children, Linda, Tom and Joanne. She and Eddie had a joke; every morning when he left for work, he would bang on her bedroom window to wake her up. She was—and is—a very dear friend.

Jeannie told me to go into the kitchen where there was butter on the counter. As I walked into the kitchen, all the cupboard doors were open and you couldn't get a toothpick in them, they were so full of food.

Then she asked me to get a drink from the fridge. That, too, was full. The freezer was full.

Cases of beer in the dining room were stacked to the ceiling. Then a knock at the back door…more groceries, box after box.

I was numb. *Where did all this come from?*

Peggy and Jean had gone door to door in our neighborhood and said they were having a pantry party for us.

I don't think a single person didn't help. I have no idea to this day how much money they collected, but there was enough food to feed an army. It was all over whelming. I felt like I was sleepwalking in a wonderful dream. So many times had been a nightmare this was so different I didn't want to wake up if it was a dream.

The little bungalow on Hayward was rocking with laughter, teasing, hugs and even crying. Neighbors coming in and out just to say hi and welcome home…some bringing cakes or other dishes…. you never visited with empty hands in those days.

The ambulance drivers from Baltimore stood there in amazement. They had never seen anything like it.

We coaxed them to stay for dinner and although they had a long drive back to Baltimore, they didn't want to leave the warm and loving feeling that was being shown.

It was so good to be home!!!

* * *

We had a very special Christmas that year. The boys were with their daddy and me. A beautiful, little, live Christmas tree filled our house with the scent of spruce. Wonderful aromas of sweet potatoes, stuffing, dumplings, turnip greens and of course turkey greeted all who came to the front door…all in preparation for a Christmas day dinner.

Our family came from Delaware. Yes, even Mrs. Buck came and, although we would never have the close relation that some daughter-in-laws and mother-in-laws have, we were cordial for Ed's sake. I tried once to talk to her about it but she made it clear that she only had room for her son in her life and that was how she wanted it. It's a shame how so much life can be lost if you don't open your heart to change. But at least she came to our house and enjoyed the Christmas holidays. It made Eddie very happy and at that time he didn't know the strained relationship existed...for his sake it was covered up.

Our house was filled with laughter and good times once again. Our local newspaper came to do a human-interest story on the man who survived being electrocuted and his first homecoming. This was a bright spot. (We didn't know it, but after the initial news story on the young man from Fruitland MD having been electrocuted on the job, they had been running articles on Eddie ever so often, giving the people in our town an up date on his progress. Everyone felt connected to the young family.)

But early January was hanging over our head. We were going to make the best of it.

We had decided that I would no longer live in Baltimore. Our sons needed their mommy more then Eddie needed me now. I was going to go up every weekend to see him, sometimes taking the boys with me. Danny was in kindergarten, and my father had taken him to school every morning...so we needed to start him in Fruitland and give him a much needed structured life ...or as close to normal as we could make it for him.

* * *

Mom and Dad had closed their shell shop for the winter. (Dad was a schoolteacher in the winter.) They had gotten so accustomed to the boys staying with them; mom would make them "paper" pancakes in the morning. It kept them very busy being parents again that when they left to come home it left such a void in their lives. They missed them like crazy! So every Friday night, they would come and get the boys, take them to their house in Delaware, and I would head for Baltimore to visit Eddie..

So the January day came for Eddie to go back to the hospital. This time he would be going to Children's Hospital in Baltimore. It was there that they did some plastic surgery and bone surgery. (He would return to this hospital about five times for extensive stays for many operations, with trips to Johns Hopkins for check-ups in between.)

* * *

One trip was very memorable . After we checked Ed into the hospital, we went to his room and settled in. The nurse came in and told us a very famous football player was across the hall. Well let me tell you.....we were football nuts...every Sunday afternoon we would be in front of our little television rooting out favorite team on. THE BALTIMORE COLTS. So when she came in to tell us that there was a player across the hall we had to know who it was. She told us it was Gino Marchetti, (for you older readers who liked football you will remember him. What a gentle giant. Gino was named the top defensive end of the NFL's first 50 years....was selected for 11 straight pro bowl games....and later inducted into the foot ball hall of fame. He was having surgery on his foot. Well, never being the shy type I immediately went across the hall to get an autograph. He was so friendly and soon we were talking like old friends.

He was so amazed with what Eddie had been through he wanted to meet him. So he came across the hallway and I introduced them. He pulled up a chair and soon they were talking like old friends. This stay in the hospital was going to be made easier by having such a great guy across the hall. When he had visitors from the team he made sure every player would be introduced to Eddie. Don Shula, the coach, and many players including Ordel Bracey and others.

Ed, being a football player in the earlier part of his life was a big fan and enjoyed that time in the hospital if that is possible. Gino also made sure they had real submarine sandwiches for lunch, the kind with the "real" Italian meats in it. So big it took two hands to wrap around it...and to eat one took a long time.   To be honest, they had some "spirits" that took the place of painkillers, and oh, they did party.

There was so much laughing between those two rooms, the nurses fussed at them. Gino threatened to buy the hospital and turn it into a Gino's, which was a fast food restaurant he had opened in the mid 1960's. Thank you Gino for making this hospital stay so much more enjoyable for Eddie.

* * *

In between surgeries, Ed was home. It was a new beginning for us—a different life. But we were just so happy to be a family again, we could face anything.

He was getting stronger every day, and he had adapted to a wheelchair. He would not use a motorized one; his arms were too strong. He was so tired of being confined...the only outing he was able to take was in an ambulance. He wanted so badly to go out for a ride, a normal ride in a normal car. But he could not get into a regular car. He was still too weak to transfer (taking a board, putting it under your buttocks and leg and sliding into a car) or pull himself into a car.

We had a little blue Ford Falcon, a mile stone because it had been a new car when we bought it. We had such fun picking it out together ...fighting over who would get to choose the color. Hmmmm....I think I got my way.

One day a group of men from Delmarva Power (the electric company he had worked for) came to the house. Eddie was sitting in his chair, and they asked him to go outside.

There, parked in our driveway, was a brand new Volkswagen Bus, complete with ramp and a hoist to pull him in.

He went for his first ride that day...sitting up and not on a stretcher. He was so excited and happy.

The next trip he made to Baltimore was in the bus and the children could go. No ambulance. It was wonderful. However, as they took our little blue Falcon away, Danny and Robbie were very upset to be losing *their* car.

* * *

In 1969 he went to Deers Head Hospital for rehabilitation. There he would learn how to dress himself all over again, to transfer to a car and to learn to drive using hand controls.

He was supposed to be an in-patient for about three months or until he could bench press 140 lbs. The first time he got on the mats, the staff put the bar...with just spoke wheels on it to keep it off his chest. He tried to press it and had such difficulty; they thought he would be there for the whole three months.

They didn't count on his having been away from his family enough that he worked hard to get back to us. He was bench pressing 145 pounds 100 times straight in three weeks.

His therapist, Mrs. Leist, told him, "Mr. Buck, I can't do any more for you. You have reached the max. Congratulations!"

And he came home.

* * *

Soon thereafter he began to drive again. At first he was very nervous behind the wheel. But after a few test runs, he was soon driving like an old pro with hand controls.   . He didn't need me to be with him every minute. It was another chapter in our daily life. This was a time for him to see how strong he was, how independent he could be, which was so important, for he had depended on me for everything.…..this was a big step on his road to recovery to feeling like the man of our house again.

* * *

We took our first vacation with the children that year. We went to the Skyline Drive and had a wonderful time, laughing and kidding.

We all had smiles on our faces from sun up to sun down.

We stopped at a motel for the night and with two small boys and energy stored, Ed told them to run into the field next door and race each other.

Danny yelled that he had lost his shoe, so we started out to the field. Ed decided he wasn't going fast enough and asked me to push him.

We were doing fine until I hit the gopher hole and Eddie did a swan dive from the chair, landing on the tall grass.

He saw the fear on my face and told Dan, "Go back to the car and get your marbles."

I looked at him like he had lost his mind.

"Don't want the people on the hills to see me down here and not doing anything. We'll play marbles while you get help."

We all laughed. Thank God for a good sense of humor.

When I went to the motel to get the clerk to help me lift him back into his chair, I found he didn't not speak much English.

When we locked arms to form a make-shift chair to lift him, Ed looked at the man and with a straight face and said, "This is the third time she has tried to kill me this trip."

I felt the man's hands go slack. I laughed and said, "Ed, tell him you are kidding

"Nooo, she has really tried three times." He said trying to keep a straight face.

After he was safely back in his chair, I told him I hoped he and the children would enjoy their trip, as I would be taken to jail.

After we got back to our room, I looked out the window ever so often to see if a police car would be turning into the motel parking lot!

We took the boys to the Luray Caverns and although Eddie couldn't go in he wanted the boys to see them. So he just sat in the car and waited for us to tour the Caverns   …go to the gift shop to get souvenirs…and let the boys run to stretch their legs. So unselfish is this guy.

What wonderful memories I have of that trip.

A routine was working out. However, Ed's lack of employment was taking its toll. He was chomping at the bit to go back to work.

It had been about two years since the accident. And although the company had stuck by him—worker's comp paid half of his salary and D.P.& L paid the other half, he was ready to return to work.

The Company had a job for him as Junior Clerk. He started back half days, building up to full time. But being a Junior Clerk was not going to be good enough for him.

Soon he decided to go to college and get some math courses under his belt. Eddie, who had hardly lifted a book in high school, whose book report I had done for him...was going to take algebra, trigonometry, calculus and accounting classes. I hoped he had not bitten off more then he could chew.

How wrong I was. He was always on top...always getting in the 90's and even then he was not happy unless he got an A.

He became an engineer field man and did a great job. But he dreamed of becoming a system operator. Since he was wheelchair bound, the company would not consider it...at least, not at first.

"Let me prove myself," he would say.

"But the stress of this job...the physical demands it takes...the shift work...this is too hard for you," they would reply.

But the Taurus in him would not let them stand in his way. He kept hounding them until they told him if he could pass the stress test and other tests, he could do it. They did not feel he could or would do it.

Now I was always there with him— to help him get dressed in the morning and there during the day and when he went to bed... if he needed me. However the *test* was for him to fly to Pittsburgh Pennsylvania, stay in a hotel, go to an office and take an 8-hour test, then get back on a plane and fly back to Salisbury *alone*. I was not allowed to go.

"That is so unfair!" I shouted.

"Honey, I can do it," He told me.

I was so scared. "What if this? What if that?"

"Believe in me. I know I can do it," he tried to reassure me.

* * *

With great fear as I packed his suitcase, I prayed that he would be able to do it. I was on pins and needle all day.

Unfortunately this took place before cell phones were popular. So I had to wait until he got to the hotel to tell me he was all right. And then the next day, I had to wait until he got home to find out how he did.

Of course, he had to wait for an opening...place his name in the running and then wait and wait....and wait, to see if his dream would finally come true.

It did, and he became a system operator, a very highly respected job in management. I was so proud of him and—even more important—he was proud of his accomplishments and his ability to prove he could do it himself.

We had moved to our new home a couple years before. I kidded my wonderful neighbors and told them we were moving *uptown*. Actually, we only moved a block away, but the house was much bigger and it was going to be made handicapped accessible. So we had to leave our little bungalow where so many happy memories were stored—memories of before the accident when life was happy and free...where Eddie taught Danny how to play baseball, trying to get him to hold the bat in his right hand and then realizing that Danny was left-handed as he watched him hit the ball over the garage. The little bungalow where he used to grab me by my heels, lift me over his back and use me for weights, making all the neighbors laugh. (I have the memory of his hanging out diapers after dark so the other men wouldn't see him…. My manly man, lying in the grass with two little boys crawling all over him. Yes, I have wonderful memories of our bungalow.

* * *

The boys were now both in school and I started substitute teaching in school—for the next three years. (I then went to work at Glen Avenue School full time; that way I would be home shortly after school and be off on the same days as our boys were. I would also have summers off with them. I worked there for nine years.)

Eddie got his job as system operator. Since his was shift work, we felt it was better for me to be home.

There were times he still needed a little help, and I needed to be there for him. So I left my job at Glen Avenue to be home with him. I took some courses and began to do Income Taxes part time. I wanted to contribute to our finances, too. But my main priority was to be available for my husband.

I was so proud of this young man. I knew there was something special about him when I met him the summer of '61, and he has proven it time and time again.

He worked as a system operator until the company moved the job to the northern division in another state. Ed was asked to either move or take a new position.

We had grandchildren, family, and a house that was perfectly handicapped accessible, so to move and start over was out of the question. So he took the position of Supervisor of maps and records. It wasn't the job he had loved so much, but he enjoyed his fellow employees and made the best of it.

In 1996 our town got its first minor league baseball team. Since both of us loved baseball, it was only fitting we get season tickets to the games.

The stadium was beautiful and our seats were right behind home plate. The young pitchers would sit in our area with their stat sheets and radar guns, taking reading on the pitches.

The Montreal Expos came to town with the same enthusiasm the people of the town offered them. It was a magical summer. We became very close to four of the young pitchers, having them over for dinner, cutting their hair and supporting them emotionally.

Two of them became our adopted sons—Troy Mattes (who is now a pitching coach for a farm team of the Orioles Baseball league) ... and Jeremy Powell (who plays professional ball for the Tokyo Giants in Japan). This you have to picture...I took them to Washington, D.C. and walked to the different museums. Here we were Troy at 6'8", Jeremy at 6'5" and me, a mere 5'2"—a strange picture walking across the mall at the Smithsonian Museum.

But what a summer we had. We enjoyed barbeque picnics. We have an above ground pool (about 4'10" deep), and these two giants cavorted around dunking each other and making waves. We had many, many laughs.

But always in the back of your mind was what's next? And it happened.

Ed was having trouble with incontinence and was getting small ulcers. It was a constant battle for him to be able to work. He went to the urologist and got the bad news.

He had precancerous tumors in the bladder.

The doctors in this area said to more-or-less go home and enjoy what time he had left.

NO WAY! We hadn't come this far only to give up now. So with the help of another paraplegic in the area and a gynecologist who went out of his way to get us the information (We thank you, Dr. Wheelless), we found a place that gave us hope.

There was nowhere in the area that would solve the problem, so we had to fly to California to the Norris Cancer Clinic at USC. There a new bladder was made from Ed's colon.

Of course, the Workers Compensation Insurance Company refused to pay, calling it cosmetic surgery. So we had to mortgage everything to pay the hospital and doctors up front, rent a hotel room for a month, rent a car for a month…and worry about it later.

There was one problem: they wanted him to go to a rehab hospital for ten days after the surgery to be monitored. He came out of the hospital with three tubes for drainage which had to be collected, measured and recorded every two-to-three hours.

We had no money for this, so I took him back to the hotel and we did it ourselves. I found out that the human body can go without sleep for quite a while.

I have to refer to my "baseball guys" at this time. Our own sons, Dan and Rob, were as worried about their dad as I was. I was so scared, because the operation did have a mortality rate and I didn't know how strong his heart was. So when I talked to our boys, I couldn't tell them how scared I was or how lonely this place was. They were worried enough and couldn't drop everything to fly out with me. They suffered such guilt…we have always been a close-knit family and leaned on each other through good and bad times. But they had families to support, small children, and responsibilities.

But I could tell my baseball guys, who called me every night to see how we were doing. I could be scared. I could be mad. I could cry or laugh. I could be me. They were my life line

The surgery was a rousing success and gave him his life back. After a month, we were on our way home…much better then before.

Now we had to go to court to fight the insurance company for the money.

The jury was out maybe 10 minutes and came back in our favor. (Later in talking to a couple of the members of the jury, they thought it was a very straightforward case and didn't understand why workers comp. insurance would fight something so necessary.)

* * *

The stress of the past year caught up with me, and I had a heart attack six months later.

It was April and we were all packed to go to Florida for spring training to see our boys. I was put in C.C.U. and after a stint was put in, I would be able to go home.

I told the doctor we were going to Florida. After <u>much</u> persuasion, he said I could go, as long as I followed his orders: NO LIFTING OR STRAINING, etc.

I promised and although Ed fought against it and questioned the doctor over and over, we left for Florida the next week.

Our roles were reversed. Ed now became caregiver, and he was wonderful at it, — although a little too strict in his orders of what I was allowed to do.

* * *

The sense of humor we share makes life so much easier to bear.

A few months after the accident, we took Dan and Rob fishing off the jetties in Ocean City, Maryland, which was about 20 miles from home. As Ed and the boys were fishing, a woman walked by staring at him.

Now Ed has scars from the fire and is missing a leg. But as you can see by the pictures, he is a very handsome man. However, this woman just kept staring at him.

She walked back and forth about four times.

Finally on her fourth time she asked, "Ahhh, catching anything?"

He lifted his stump and said, "Yup, shark."

After she walked away, we reeled in laughter.

Most of the time people are genuine in their desire to understand what happened to him…especially children. And to them he is most gracious. He explains what happened to him and how lucky he is to still be here. But he has little patience with gawkers. Always with humor he tries to put them in their place.

* * *

After our decision not to move, he became the supervisor of Maps and Records, where he stayed there until his retirement on March 1, 1998, after almost 33 years with the company.

With Ed as a paraplegic, life has been like a roller coaster ride. Everything can be going wonderfully and then boom! You are on a downward spiral.

This could be a pressure area or breakdown of the skin, which means bed rest for days or even weeks. Then it might be a kidney infection, which is prevalent among paraplegics or quadriplegics. Legs and feet swelling....a bump that is not felt but turns into a doctor's visit and bed rest or, at the worst, surgery.

Planning is not really an option. Vacations are called off at the last minute many, many times. We just have to grab life and run with it.

So, we have been on a roller coaster ride. But you know, I wouldn't change that ride for anything.

And now today, forty-six years later—yes, forty-six years, we are both enjoying life and what it has to offer. There are times we wonder what if....but we are both so appreciative of the years we have had and what lies ahead, we can't look back.

We travel as much as possible, having gone as far north as Maine, south to Florida, and west to California ....plus the fun of cruising.

As the years have progressed, I have taken up new hobby writing. I now write children's books, both whimsical and religious. I have one novel finished and published and am working on my second.

However, I put that one on hold to write my portion of Ed's story, one that I felt had to be told and a legacy for our children and a book telling others that you can survive great odds and make a wonderful life. You know, take the lemons and make lemonade.

Today in addition to our four grandchildren...our two wonderful sons, a fantastic daughter, (okay, to be politically correct, daughter-in-law) Laraine, we have two cats—K.C. and Sadie, and one rottenly spoiled Brittany spaniel, Bentley.

Yes, life has been a roller coaster ride, filled with up times and down times. But to tell you the truth, I wouldn't have gotten off that ride for anything.

I still love that man so much—my husband, best friend, inspiration, lover...and yes, the man who was....

Dying To Survive.

Clara Hammie's Story

As I stood in the doorway of a patient's room observing all the commotion coming from room 217, one of the staff nurses came down the hall.

"What was going on in that room?" I asked.

She shook her head sadly. "There is a very sick patient in there," she told me "He has sustained burns over 80% of his body from an electrical accident

When I asked her if she thought he was going to make it, she said that only God knew that answer.

I went back into my patient's room and the nurse continued her journey down the hall. I immediately felt a strong sense of compassion for the burn patient.

The patient I was taking care of at this time had also been burned and was in a great deal of pain. However he had only sustained burns on both arms and legs—not nearly as bad as the man in Halsted 217. I had been taking care of this man for two months; he was recovering very well from his burns since he had skin grafts to all extremities.

80% burns, I was thinking as I prepared to change my patient's dressings. I loved being a nurse and especially liked working as a private duty nurse. That way I could give the kind of nursing care I felt my patients deserved.

I knew from early childhood that I wanted to be a nurse. I pretended to take care of my baby dolls after they had had "surgery".

I spent two years in the United States Women's Army Corps as a medic and loved every minute of it. While in the military, I heard about Johns Hopkins Hospital and vowed to work there one day.

While I was in the military, I met and married a young man by the name of David Hammie. He was discharged first and successfully talked me out of re-enlisting when my time was up. After many painful days of indecision, I finally agreed not to re-enlist and was honorably discharged as a Specialist 5th Class. I regretted that decision, but I was trying to be a dutiful wife.

We spent a little over two years in Atlantic City both working in the hospital. Atlantic City Hospital wouldn't recognize my credentials as a medic from the Army. Being the feisty and unbeatable person I am, I put my pride and disappointment aside and worked as a nurse's aide until I enrolled in the Licensed Practical Nurse program.

I passed all my courses, graduating number one in my class and making 711 on the nurse's boards. (The highest score anyone can make is 800.) I worked as a nurse until David decided to finish his college education at Morgan State College in Baltimore, Maryland.

* * *

I answered an ad that I saw in an RN magazine for nurses at Johns Hopkins Hospital and was hired as a staff nurse in the Halsted Surgical Building.

I was happy and loved my new job. The registered nurse and four technicians I worked with bonded and we became quite a team on the 3 to 11 shift. Sadly the good working relationship came to a screeching halt after Barbara, the RN, married and moved away.

I put up with the personalities of the registered nurses who came on the floor to work with me. It didn't matter to the doctors that I wasn't a registered nurse; they looked to me to make sure everything was done for their patients. (Unfortunately, the registered nurse rescinded that and made it obvious to me. After a very serious altercation with the registered nurse concerning a patient, I knew I couldn't take it any longer.)

After talking with Ms. Phyllis Conner, the department head and person who hired me, I resigned from the staff duty. I worked for the 30 days notice and then joined Central Directory of Nurses where Ms. Conner put me to work as a private duty nurse.

I had enjoyed being a staff nurse, but giving one-on-one nursing care gave me such a sense of accomplishment. I was able to give the kind of nursing care I wanted to give as a staff nurse but couldn't.

I didn't know the day I talked to the staff nurse about Mr. Edward Buck that I would soon be embarking on a journey with that man and his wife that would last over three decades.

* * *

I later found out that Phyllis Conner had made several phone calls one morning, trying to find a replacement for the nurse taking care of Mr. Buck. He was so sick and required so much work that every nurse who had worked with him stayed no more than two days. Phyllis had exhausted all her resources and could only think of one person who she felt would stay with Mr. Buck, and that was me. But I was already working with a patient.

My patient was doing very well, and the doctors would probably take away his private duty nurse. So Phyllis Conner decided to at least ask me if I would take Mr. Buck on as a patient. All I could do was say yes or no.

I had just finished changing my patient's dressings and was cleaning up when Ms. Connors entered my room. We exchanged greetings. She asked my patient, Mr. Little, how he was doing.

He replied, "Thanks to God, his doctors, and his nurse, I am doing very well. If there are any better nurses, God has them up there with Him."

His statement made me very proud, especially when Ms. Connors said that she agreed with him and was very pleased to hear that vote of confidence from him.

She asked me if we could take a break because she wanted to talk to me about something. I told her I would meet her in the kitchen as soon as I put Mr. Little's favorite record on the record player.

Conner left the room and I searched through a pile of records and found Mahelia Jackson's greatest gospel song. When the music began playing, Mr. Little settled back on his pillows and closed his eyes as he listened to the lady's sweet, melodic voice.

* * *

I joined Ms. Connors in the kitchen, where I poured myself a cup of coffee and retrieved a Danish roll from the covered container.

Ms. Connors got right to the point. "Although I know you are busy, I am having an awful time trying to keep nurses on with a patient in room 217, Mr. Edward Buck. He had a terrible accident while working and sustained 80% electrical burns over his body. He is very critical and requires a lot of work."

I looked at her as she took another sip of her coffee and continued, "Would you please consider taking him on as a patient. I need someone with your experience in taking care of burn patients."

She had spoken to the doctors and they agreed that I would be perfect. They were planning to stop Mr. Little's nursing care sometime next week anyway, since he was doing so well and that she could get coverage for him.

"I can't find anyone who will take Mr. Buck's case," she said, her voice pleading for help.

"I will do it," I told her. I appreciate your confidence in my abilities to take care of such a critical case. When do you want me to start?"

She told me that the nurse with Mr. Buck now had agreed to stay on through to the next day. I hadn't had a day off in over two weeks and was exhausted, however she wanted me to take the next day off and come in the following morning. But in the meantime, she asked me to talk to the nurse who was on with him now and read his chart to familiarize myself with his case.

She complimented me, "You're an excellent nurse with any patient that you care for. I really appreciate you taking this case."

She asked me if I wanted her to talk to Mr. Little about my leaving. I told her no that I would do it.

We talked about Mr. Buck until we finished our coffee and buns. Then Ms. Connors went to the charge nurse and Mr. Buck's nurse to tell them the news.

When I returned to his room, Mr. Little asked, "Is everything okay?

"Yes, however, Ms. Conner asked me take another case starting the day after tomorrow. Today is going to be my last day with you. Another nurse will be taking my place in the morning so that I can have tomorrow off."

He said, "No other nurse could take your place, but understood. Thank you for taking such good care of me the last two months."

He complimented me by telling me I was an excellent nurse with a very kind heart. And through all his pain, I managed to make him smile and even laugh sometimes. He told me that he felt my talents as a nurse were God-given. He told me that he would miss me very much and hoped that my new patient would recover from his injuries.

* * *

The remainder of that day, my patient and I enjoyed each other's company, as we usually did. I spoke to Mr. Buck's nurse, peeked into the room and then I read his chart.

At 6:30 p.m. my relief nurse arrived and we went into the kitchen to look at reports.

Mr. Little gave me a big hug and kissed my cheek when I was getting ready to leave the room. We both had tears in our eyes.

* * *

I arrived on duty at 6:15 AM the next morning. I pulled Mr. Buck's chart and read the doctor's history and physical notes from the previous day while sipping coffee and eating a cornbread muffin. Then I read doctors orders for the day.

At 6:35 AM, I knocked lightly on the door and then introduced myself to the night nurse, Mr. Owens, who gave me his report. "I don't think you will be on this assignment very long, because there is no way Mr. Buck can survive the severity of his burns."

I got very angry, because I don't like working with people who have negative thoughts.

"Why did you say that?" I snapped. "Do you know more about this man's survival than God does?"

I could tell he didn't like what I said or the sound of my voice.

"No I don't," he retorted. "I'll see you tonight," he growled. —

I didn't care. *He doesn't walk on water, so how does he know for sure whether Mr. Buck will live or die?* It was our job to do our best with a positive attitude to see that he did. A patient can pick up on a nurse's attitude, and a positive one brings forth a positive response from the patient. Or at least, that is how I strongly feel.

* * *

With gown, mask, cap and gloves on, I approached Mr. Buck's bed quietly. He was asleep. I looked at the man lying in the bed with IVs in all extremities and his body covered with dressings.

I could barely see his chest rise and fall in the dimly lit room; I could see that he was a very handsome man, tall and well built.

I didn't like the way his dressings looked. They weren't put on neatly at all; they looked sloppy. I wasn't too surprised because of Mr. Owens' attitude about Mr. Buck's survival.

As I watched my patient sleeping, I was thinking, *Dear God, what pain this man must be going through. He was left in here for a reason, and I pray you give the doctors and me the knowledge to help keep him alive, because he has a lot to live for.*

I understood he had a wife and two small children. Someone had made a list of supplies, so I checked it against what he had; everything was there that the doctors would need.

I was checking the intravenous solution in Mr. Buck's legs when he opened his eyes.

"Good morning," I greeted. "My name is Clara Hammie and I will be your day nurse until 7 p.m."

We were in very sterile conditions. And so with my mask on, I knew he couldn't know what I looked like. Carefully I lowered my mask, holding my breath, so he could see my face. All he got to see were people with masks on.

I knew he must be a little confused. I smiled at him and he tried to return my smile but it hurt his face.

I told him, "Mr. Buck, as I said, my name is Clara Hammie, but my friends call me Hammie.

He said, "Will you please call me Ed?"

He told me that his wife, Michelle, would be there at eight o'clock, but everyone calls her Micki.

I asked him if he and Michelle had any children. He told me they had two little boys whose names were Danny and Robbie. Danny was five and Robbie was two.

While we continued to exchange small talk, I checked his vital signs and temperature. At 7:30 a.m. someone knocked lightly on the door and entered the room.

It was then that I met Dr. Michael Jabaley, Ed's head plastic surgeon. I introduced myself and told him that I was Mr. Buck's day nurse until 7 p.m., that his temperature was slightly elevated, but his other vital signs were all within normal range.

I handed him Ed's special chart. He told me that I had come very highly recommended and that was what Mr. Buck needed—a well qualified nurse. He told me that every morning he would do rounds to check all his burns sites. He would leave an order for the night nurse to wash off the ointment and cover him in sterile towels. And after his rounds, Mr. Buck would be going to physical therapy and put in what was called the Hubbard tank. This tank would loosen any skin that needed debrieding. Some of this third degree burns might need to be surgically debrieded.

He told me that when I brought him back to his room, I needed to reapply the sulfamyolin ointment and sterile dressings. He then handed me Ed's special chart.

Dr. Jabaley and one of the residents began cutting away Ed's dressings on his legs first. I had a sterile towel ready for them to place his legs on after they had removed the dressings.

I thought my last patient's burns were severe, but there was no comparison between his and Ed's.

I glanced at Dr. Jabaley's face and could tell from his eyes and the frown on his forehead that he didn't like what he was seeing. The ointment wasn't spread smoothly over the burn sites and applied too thickly.

I pulled the bedside table over Ed's chest, opened a sterile basin, poured saline in it and dropped several packs of 4 x 4s in the saline.

The doctors changed sterile gloves and washed off the ointment. Most of the burns were second degree, which accounted for all the loss of precious body fluids.

Ed grimaced with pain as I tried very hard to conceal my feelings. But I thought, *oh my God, the pain Ed must be feeling.*

Dr. Jabaley told him he was so sorry to have to put him through all of this, but he had to see how the burns were healing. He told him that the second-degree burns were nice and pink with no signs of infection. The third-degree burns would have to be surgically debrieded but not for a few weeks. They worked on his other burn sites next and finish by culturing each extremity.

I asked Dr. Jabaley if he wanted me to culture his burn sites before we went down to physical therapy each morning. He told me that was a brilliant idea, and that the lab would be doing blood work each morning and in the evening.

He said, "We have to keep on top of his electrolytes, since he's losing so much fluid from the second degree site. I will write his orders outside and the floor nurse will tell you what they are" He looked at me and said, "Welcome aboard, Mrs. Hammie," as he and his crew left the room.

* * *

`My best friend, Faye, was the charge nurse. She stuck her head in the door and said she had Mr. Buck's new orders. She would call physical therapy and bring his meds, IV solutions and injections.

As I thanked her, I saw a pretty petite lady talking to Dr. Jabaley and assumed it was Ed's wife, Micki. However after I studied her, I decided she should be called Michelle.

She came in a few minutes later dressed in the sterile paraphernalia.

I said, "Good Morning" and introduced myself. I asked her a question and addressed her as Mrs. Buck.

"Oh, please, call me Micki," she said warmly.

I told her she looked like a Michelle and we agreed that was what I would call her. I in turn told her to call me Hammie.

She quickly walked over to her husband and greeted him.

"How was your night?" she asked.

He told her he was still in a lot of pain. Then he asked her if she had spoken to their sons.

She assured him she had and that they sent bunches of kisses and lots of love, as well as Dee and her family sent theirs.

I let Michelle help Ed with his breakfast, although it was painful for him to eat. And at 10:00 I took him down to physical therapy for the Hubbard Tank.

The therapist showed me how to scrub his burn sites with a soft brush while he cut away the dead tissue as it sloughed off.

Ed cried out in pain and agony during the bath. My heart went out to him, but I knew it had to be done.

He was in the tank for thirty minutes, but I'm sure it seemed like hours to him. As soon as I got Ed back to his room I reapplied the ointment to his burn sites. He eventually went to sleep.

The end of my fist day finally came and I was bone tired. The bus ride home helped me relax, but I was thinking about my new patient and his wife.

They were so young. He was 25 and she was 24. *How in the world will their marriage survive such a trial? I could tell they loved each other so very much by the way they talked to each other, and how he comes alive as soon as she walks in. What will happen to her if he dies?* God left this man here for a reason but I had never heard of anyone who sustained burns of such magnitude survive.

Michelle was a different kind of person. She was always so optimistic, always showing a positive approach. I sometimes wondered if that was how she really felt on the inside.

* * *

There was a very special doctor who became friends with Ed and Michelle. His name was Dr. Iams. He was very pessimistic about Ed's outcome for survival, having seen patients with burns of less severity die shortly after admittance. So he was always trying to get Michelle to see the reality of the situation.

He would tell her not to get her hopes up, because some of the burn sites had already become infected, and he feared pneumonia would develop which would be fatal. He was also afraid Ed's heart would give out from all the infection in his body.

But no matter what he said to her, Michelle remained optimistic.

Since Michelle was going to be in the room every day, I decided to give her something to do to make her feel useful. I taught her how to wash, dry and wrap the instruments, dressings, towels and bowls that the doctors used every day. Doing that, along with helping Ed try to eat and encourage each mouth full—as he was losing weight and didn't want to eat because of pain, Michelle felt apart of his recovery.

I knew I was doing my treatments as Dr. Jabaley had prescribed, but I wasn't so sure that Mr. Owens was. I came on duty an hour early one morning before he could remove his dressings and saw that they looked greenish in color. (My excuse to Mr. Owens was that I came in early to catch up on reading Ed's chart…something I couldn't do during the day.)

I didn't like reporting another nurse, but I told Ms. Conner what I had seen earlier that morning when she made her rounds. Together we decided that I would mark my dressings before putting them on for the last time before I left for the night and also mark the bed linens, which were to be changed frequently due to the oozing wounds.

The next morning Ms. Conner and I entered Ed's room early just as Mr. Owens was removing Ed's dressings, much to his surprise. He was shocked to see the orange mark I had put on during the last dressing change the night before and the orange mark on the bed linen tucked way under the mattress.

Needless to say, Ms. Conner took Mr. Owens out of the room and promptly fired him. No one was going to put my patient in danger, as long as I had any say in the matter.

I requested and got Mrs. Plocheck to replace him. We had worked together many times, and I trusted her judgment and skills.

Ed began having horrendous nightmares and I couldn't understand why. He would cry out in his sleep for someone to leave him alone. But he would never explain what he was dreaming.

One day as I was going about my normal duties, he asked to speak to Michelle alone. I left them in private, just standing outside the door, watching from the little window to make sure he was alright. (He had to be watched every minute for fear of what might happen. When one of us left the room, someone else was there to replace us.)

After a few minutes, Michelle motioned for me to come back in. Then she asked if we could have lunch together.

I didn't know what to expect but told her that would be fine.

At my lunch break when another nurse came in to relieve me, we went to the cafeteria. It was then Michelle proceeded to tell me why Ed was having those nightmares.

When he was a young boy, he had gotten a new bicycle for Christmas. As he was out riding, a group of Negro boys had beaten him up and taken his bike. Michelle explained that although he didn't hate Negroes, he just didn't trust them... that being in a segregated school; he didn't have any other contact with them.

But now that he met me and was finding himself caring so deeply, he was afraid he would say something that would offend me during the times he was hallucinating from the drugs.

I told Michelle that I was so glad she had told me this story and that I would take care of things after lunch. I think we were both relieved, for Ed could come to grips with his fears and I now could understand the nightmares and handle them accordingly.

* * *

Michelle went into the room first to tell Ed that we had had a talk and all was fine. I went in next and asked Michelle to give us a few minutes alone.

She left the room and I told Ed that I was very sorry he had had such a bad experience. I asked him how the incident had affected his feeling toward Negroes.

He explained that he didn't hate them but didn't trust them, just as Michelle said. But since meeting me and being with me everyday, he was afraid he might say something to hurt me.

When I told him Michelle had told me of his fears. I could see relief in his face.

I told him I grew up in a totally segregated town. The Negroes couldn't eat in any restaurant or any lunch counter. We could not try on any clothes and had to sit in the balcony at the theater. I told him that, thank God, I had parents who taught us that there was good and bad in all races, even the Negro race. Look at the character of the individual and not his color.

When I left home, I never forgot what my parents taught me. Through the years, I've met and made friends with both Negroes and white people. I told him I wanted him to speak about the incident to the psychiatrist and he could help him work through the negative feelings so he wouldn't have the nightmares any more.

I told him to not worry about hurting my feelings. I was just glad I knew about the incident. And now if he didn't do what I wanted, I was going to smack his white ass.

At that point, Michelle came back into the room to gales of laughter. Never again was there any tension in this room about race. (Ed did talk to the doctor about it and the doctor explained that he was experiencing a form of posttraumatic stress syndrome. His accident caused the unpleasant memories to come flooding back due to his surrounding.)

The days blurred into weeks for both all of us. I had worked 38 days straight and needed a day off badly. Ms. Conner found a nurse to relieve me for two days.

Finally Dr. Jabaley stopped the Hubbard Tank treatments, and Ed was glad. Mrs. Plocheck and I would still put him in a portable tub in his room for his bath.

Ed and I would argue every day about the water being too warm for him. With so much of his surface skin gone, the water felt hot to him, but to me it felt cool. Playfully he would threaten to whip me when he could get out of bed, and I would dare him and threaten to whip his white ass anytime he tried.

The staff would hear us arguing and it made the day so much brighter on Halsted Two.

The infections began to clear up and Dr. Jabaley began talking about debrieding his third-degree burns. Our care was paying off.

* * *

I did the one thing a private duty nurse should never do: I became emotionally involved with both my patient and his wife.

At night when I got home from work, I would itch. I discussed this situation with Dr. Jabaley and he prescribed something for the itching. He told me I had become too close to Ed and Michelle, but he assured me that he understood how that could happen. He, too, was becoming very attached to them.

He also suggested a hot bath and a hot toddy before taking the medicine.

I remembered my Sergeant telling my class that one day in order to help a patient, it might be necessary to inflict pain upon them. This might affect them emotionally, but they had to suck it up and know in their hearts that we were helping our patients.

This is what I was experiencing. Some days were worse then others, depending on how Ed responded to the pain I was inflicting as I scrubbed and debrieded his burns. One day it got so bad for him that when I finished his bath and dressings, I went to the bathroom and cried *big time*.

* * *

By this time, Michelle and I had become good friends. However, I noticed she was also losing weight at an alarming rate.

I knew things were not good at the apartment where she was living. Their two small boys and Ed's mother were living with her. Evidently Ed's mother could not—or would not—accept the responsibility of staying with the boys while Michelle helped Ed in the hospital

The doctors had told her how important it was for some family member to be with him as much as possible every day. His mother wouldn't come to the hospital because it was too painful for her to see her son in this condition, which is totally understandable.

I could see that Michelle's nerves were at a breaking point; however, any time I would mention this to her, she would always say she was fine. I think we both knew she was not telling the truth.

I talked to Dr. Jabaley about this because, frankly, I was worried she might have a nervous breakdown. He set up an appointment for her to see a psychiatrist, which she did reluctantly.

After the meeting, I could see she had been crying, something I had never seen her do. That was good.

I put my arm around her shoulder and told her she had to do something about the home situation. She couldn't go on like this. She agreed and left the room to call her parents about taking the boys so she could continue helping Ed.

Over the next several days I could see her improving. I know she missed her sons so much, but her need was to be with her husband.

Ed was improving. One by one, the IV's were coming out.

He had lost a lot of weight and was given anything and everything he wanted to eat and drink. To keep his kidney's functioning after the Foley catheter was removed, he had to drink beer three times a day. He told me that he had enjoyed an occasional beer before the accident but having to drink so many of them daily now tasted like medicine to him.

Even though he was so horribly injured, he had a great sense of humor and the student nurses would fight over who got to take him for different tests. The interns enjoyed teasing with him, so it was a room they all enjoyed visiting.

Once Ed's family members, friends and co-workers found out he needed to gain weight, they brought him baked goodies. He had so much food in his room that it was known as Buck's bakery. He shared everything with all the nurses, doctors, starving interns, student nurses, orderlies, and cleaning crew. They all knew where good snacks could be found.

Gradually Ed was allowed to sit up on the side of the bed three times a day. The first time he sat up, he felt so dizzy.

"I think my eyeballs are rotating completely around inside my head," he said. Then he laughed.

I told him, "I've never heard of such a thing happening. But with you, anything is possible!"

The doctors were preparing him to get up and walk. After a week of working him into a sitting position, I stood him up beside the bed. Of course, the first day he felt lightheaded, but that soon passed.

Michelle helped me pin a towel around his groin area so he wouldn't feel embarrassed. We placed towels over the mirror and other areas so he wouldn't be able to look in the mirror and see his burns. I didn't think he was ready for that.

Three days later I spread a sterile sheet on the floor and he walked from his bed to a large stuffed chair, covered with a sterile sheet. Finally he walked from the chair to the door and felt extremely proud of his accomplishment.

Even though Michelle could see the improvement in Ed's condition, it was hard for her to completely relax. I allowed her to walk beside him after she felt comfortable that he could walk without being helped. Anything Michelle could do for her husband boosted both her and his morale, and I wasn't about to deny them that pleasure.

Dr. Jabaley was going to be away from the hospital to take his family on a short vacation to Williamsburg, He assured us all that he would be in touch with the hospital every day.

The next day a young intern came in, and—against our wishes—gave Ed a tetanus shot. I questioned him that it was not in the orders, but he told me he did not want to compound Ed's problem with lockjaw.

A couple of days later, Ed began to have problems picking up his right foot while he was walking. The electricity had entered his left hand and ran diagonally across his body and exited out through his right foot.

When I noticed him dragging his foot, I asked him if it hurt to walk on it. He told me that it didn't, but it felt like it weighed a ton. He said it didn't feel like that when he first started walking.

By the fourth day the numbness and heavy feeling had moved up Ed's entire right leg. He had only walked a short distance when he had to sit down.

I told him he was just being lazy that day and to try to walk to the door. But when I tried to get him up, he couldn't.

I thought he was kidding at first, because he was such a prankster. But when he kept trying and couldn't get up, I knew he was telling the truth, especially when I saw the tears in his eyes.

I got a male nurse and orderly to put him back in bed. He dozed off to sleep immediately.

I kept thinking, *Something is definitely wrong.* I got a sterile safety pin and pricked Ed's body from the bottom of his right foot upward toward his chest. He didn't respond to the pin prick until I got just above the nipple.

By then he couldn't move his arms and was having trouble breathing. I could see the panic on Michelle's face as I stuck my head out the door and asked Faye to page the doctors stat and I asked for a tracheotomy tray.

Ed's doctors came running to his room. They asked Michelle to leave the room for a little bit. Then I told them what had happened.

One of the doctors repeated the pin prick and they looked at each other with concern. One doctor left the room and called a neurologist stat.

After his arrival and examination, he assessed that Ed has developed T6 paralysis, which left him without feeling from his feet to above his nipples. The neurologist ordered a respirator to be on stand-by and saw that I already had the tracheotomy set up in the room. He told me it was a good call to already have it there, in case we needed it. He told me not to hesitate to call if his breathing became too labored.

Soon after this, Michelle told me about her experience with the statue of Jesus in the rotunda at the entrance of the hospital. Suddenly her faith that Ed would be coming home got to be so strong. The doctors tried to prepare her for what might happen; but to their dismay, she would always tell them that Ed would be going home with her and their children.

The following Monday morning, Michelle came into the room to find Dr. Jabaley standing at Ed's bedside looking very sad and rubbing his forehead. He felt so badly about being out of town when the paralysis set in, and Ed was reassuring the doctor that is was not his fault.

Ed asked, "Will it go away?"

Dr. Jabaley answered, "I honestly don't know. We're not one hundred percent sure of why it happened. We will be running tests on you."

He hugged Michelle and left the room.

The two of them talked, and Ed asked her what would happen if he couldn't walk. She told him that together they could face anything and they would deal with whatever came.

I have never seen two people who loved each other more.

* * *

Ed's right foot got worse and literally began to rot away. He began to spike a fever. The doctor's were talking about amputation to save his life.

At this same time, I received a phone call from my mother in North Carolina. My father was sick and in the hospital; I needed to go home.

Ms. Conner found a replacement for me and I flew home.

My father's condition improved slowly and I felt much better. I was always daddy's girl. In the meantime, back in Baltimore, someone teased Ed and told him that I wasn't coming back to take care of him anymore. He got very upset and angry. (Ed is not one for changes. His appetite was not good to begin with, and now he began to lose weight again)

One day he raised so much hell to talk to me by phone that they had to cover him with a sterile sheet and wheel his bed across the hall to make a call to North Carolina. I was just leaving the house when my mother yelled out the window that I had a long distance call from the hospital in Baltimore.

I answered and heard Ed's quivering voice. He shouted into the phone, "Someone — told me you're not coming back to take care of me. I need you!" -

I said, "Calm down before you make yourself sicker! I don't know who told you that, but it's not true. My father is doing much better and I'll be there in a few days."

He said, "If you don't, I'm not going to fight any more and just die."

"I'm not lying, Ed. I *will* be coming back. Promise me that you'll keep fighting. We have come too far."

"Do you promise?" he asked. -

"I assure you, I'll be back soon. Now, let me speak with Michelle.—

When she came on the line, I asked her who in the hell said I was not coming back. She told me that the nurse started it as a joke to get him to do what she wanted. They told him that if he didn't cooperate, they were going to tell you not to come back, but he took it the wrong way and didn't believe they were teasing then.

"He thought they were trying to tell him that you were not coming back," she said. "He needed to hear it from you personally."

She asked me how my father was and I told her to tell everyone that he was doing very well and that I would be taking him home soon.

* * *

Two days later, Ed lapsed into a coma. Dr. Jabaley, who was in the operating room just finishing up surgery, was called stat to Ed's room. When he assessed the situation, he knew that gangrene was there and Ed was now septic.

Michelle called me in North Carolina, just after they took him to the O.R. and I could hear crying.

"It's done," she sobbed. "Ed has lapsed into a coma. They're on the way to remove his foot." She was crying so hard.

"Oh, Michelle, I'm so sorry," I tried to comfort. "Is someone from your family coming to be with you?"

"No, no one is here or is coming. But just taking to you helps," she said. "I can hold on until you get back.

I told her, "I am bringing my father home on Sunday and will be leaving here the end of the following week to come home. I know that God is with you."

After I hung up the phone my mother pointed out how attached I was to my patient and his wife. I told her that I was, against my better judgment. I told my mother how sorry I was that Michelle was by herself going through this. "Michelle spends every day at the hospital with Ed until at least 5 o'clock. After that, she is all alone in the apartment where she is staying until the next morning until it starts all over."

My mother looked at me and told me, "Clara Baldwin Hammie, don't ever change. Continue caring for your patients with your heart. God has given you a gift, and you have to use it to the max."

I promised I would.

* * *

On Friday my father said that my mother had told him about my patient in Baltimore who so depended on me.

"Go back to take care of Ed," he said.

"Daddy, are you sure?"

"I'm very sure," he answered. "I'm very proud of your accomplishments as a nurse and woman. God has given you a special gift. Continue to use it wisely."

* * *

I called Ms. Conner and told her I'd be back to work on Monday morning, but not to say anything to Michelle or Ed. I wanted to surprise them.

I flew back to Baltimore on Saturday. David, my husband, had missed me terribly, as I had him, and I was glad to be back home.

Ed was asleep when I opened the door and took the report from the night nurse. I was pleased to read that, after the amputation and massive dose of antibiotics, Ed's blood work was much better.

Then as I was checking my supplies with my back to him, Ed woke up. He gave out a big shout loud enough for the whole staff to hear on all of Halsted Two. He told me to give him a big hug from my cute self.

It was so good to hear him so chipper. He felt secure again and was full of the devil.

"Do you know how spoiled you've become?" I asked. "I wonder whose fault it is—mine or Michelle's."

He laughed. "Both! I am a sick man and require lots of attention and care."

"Well, you will be starting physical therapy, and then we'll see how much attention and care you will get from me. You will be doing a lot more for yourself."

Just then, the door opened and Michelle rushed in, giving me a big hug.

"We are so glad to see you!" she exclaimed.

She told me my friend, Mr. Ed, had to take drastic measures to get me back.

"From what I hear from Faye and some of the other nurses, I have trained you too well," I teased. "I understand that you have given the other nurses a fit because they did not do some of the things like I do."

Michelle laughed. "I confess! Maybe I was a bit critical of the way some things were done. But Eddie has been through so much and you have his treatment down to a science. So maybe you have taught me too well!"

We all got a good laugh out of that. But to me that was a very high compliment.

* * *

One day, Dr. Jabaley informed us all that Ed was going to be presented on grand rounds the following Friday. Physicians from Washington, D.C., Boston, North Carolina and New York would be in attendance.

We all got a little excited.

I asked, "Dr. Jabaley. Will I have to say anything?"

He nodded. "There will be some questions for you, but I'm not worried about your answers.

I wasn't as sure as he was.

After he left, we all talked about the grand rounds.

Ed said, "I'm going to tell all of the doctors how badly you have treated me!"

"If you do, I'll knock you off the bed!" I jokingly threatened.

* * *

On Friday Ed's bed was wheeled onto a stage. Michelle sat down front and I sat beside the bed with Ed.

I was very nervous looking out at the sea of white coats.

Dr. Jabaley approached the podium. The room got very quiet as he gave a detailed description of Ed's accident and his case.

The neurologist spoke next about his myelitis, followed by the orthopedic surgeon, who spoke about his amputations. The psychiatrist spoke last.

Each specialist had twenty minutes to answer questions posed by the doctors in the theater. At the end of the question and answer period, Dr. Jabaley stood and said, "Ladies and gentlemen I have the privilege and honor of presenting to you our miracle patient, Mr. Ed Buck and his day nurse, Mrs. Clara Hammie.

Everyone stood and gave Ed a thunderous applause. I glanced down at Michelle, who was smiling proudly.

Ed reached for my hand and I gripped it lightly and smiled down at him.

I was asked several questions first. I tried to answer them professionally from a nurse's point of view.

Finally it was Ed's turn. At one point he became a bit overcome and emotional, especially when he mentioned the support he had received from his loving wife, Michelle.

Dr. Jabaley motioned for her to stand, and she received an enthusiastic round of applause.

Dr. Jabaley saw that Ed was starting to get tired and asked the doctors to conclude the questioning.

After rounds were over; several doctors spoke to Ed, Michelle and me and shook Ed's hand as they left the room. That was a memorable moment for all of us.

* * *

Ed was recovering from his amputation well. Initially he was on a circular electric bed when I returned from North Carolina. But two weeks later, he was put back on a water bed.

His paralysis had not improved. It was still at T6 but had no trouble moving his arms or breathing.

The doctors began skin grafting to Ed's legs first after his cultures came back negative. The physical therapist came to his room to begin strength training to his upper extremities.

–Thanksgiving was fast approaching. Ed was doing very well and his upper body strength was getting much better.

Unbeknownst to me, Ed and Michelle—with the help of the floor staff, decided to have a surprise birthday party on November 21st for me.

On the morning of my birthday, I went into Ed's room as I always did and bounced him on his waterbed as he protested, although he was laughing. Ed was now off protective isolation, so no sterile preparation was needed.

To get me out of the room, Ms. Conner arranged for me to have a long lunch. When I returned to the floor after having an hour lunch break, I opened Ed's door to shouts of "HAPPY BIRTHDAY!!!"

I was so surprised and touched I had tears in my eyes.

Ed and Michelle game me a rust colored skirt and sweater to match with a white blouse. They had cake and ice cream for everyone, including the doctors.

Ed had a big, big laugh because for the first time, I was at a loss for words.

Ms. Conner said that in all her years as department head, never had a patient and family given their nurse a surprise birthday celebration. NEVER. She told me that the Bucks must really love me, to which Ed and Michelle piped up that yes they did. They loved me so much.

I then had tears running down my face.

Yes, I had broken all the rules of a private duty nurse, especially the one that warns us not to become too emotionally attached to our patients. I loved them both so much, and I thanked them for the surprise birthday party...it *was* a surprise.

* * *

We all knew that one day I would have to leave him as his private duty nurse, but neither of us were prepared when it happened.-

Dr. Jabaley wanted to see how Ed would do without a nurse before sending him home, so he was putting him in a ward.

The last day with Ed was very emotional for us. Neither of us tried to hide our tears as I prepared to leave at the end of my shift.

No matter where I was in the hospital, I stopped by every day to see Ed. He was doing very well, but we missed each other terribly.

After over five months he and Michelle got to go home for Christmas.

* * *

The following summer I went to Fruitland to visit with them. What a joyous reunion. I spent a week with them.

Several years later, Ed and Michelle were on vacation and came through Greensboro, North Carolina to visit with me.... David and I had divorced years before, and I was remarried to John Leake.

We met at a motel off Lee Street and had lunch at Quincy's. That was another glorious day spent with my two friends.

Even though over three decades have passed, I have stayed in touch with Ed and Michelle by phone and e-mail. When I have been asked what was my most interesting case I had while doing private duty, I don't hesitate to say taking care of Mr. Edward Buck.

Initially I worked 38 days straight with Ed before taking a day off. I also feel his case has been the most rewarding. He is a fighter and also has a very loving wife, who has stood by his side every step of the way. (Michelle has thanked God many nights for sparing Ed's life.)

When Ed wanted to give up, I wouldn't let him. And when he was too tired to fight, God carried him in his loving arms.

On a personal note, I, Clara Hammie, want to say, "Fight on, my friend. You have turned your scars into stars. Always remember that God loves you and Michelle, and so do I.

I'm very proud to have known both of you all these years. Each of us has felt God's love in different ways. Until we meet again face to face, I will always be your Hammie, your nurse and your FRIEND."